# Read This for Inspiration

## Simple Sparks to Ignite Your Life

ASHLY PEREZ

CLARKSON POTTER/PUBLISHERS

NEW YORK

Copyright © 2020 by Ashly Perez

All rights reserved.

Published in the United States by Clarkson Potter/Publishers, an imprint
of Random House, a division of Penguin Random House LLC, New York.
clarksonpotter.com

CLARKSON POTTER is a trademark and POTTER with colophon is
a registered trademark of Penguin Random House LLC.

Library of Congress Cataloging-in-Publication Data
Names: Perez, Ashly, author.
Title: Read this for inspiration : simple sparks to ignite your life /
   Ashly Perez.
Description: New York : Clarkson Potter, 2020. |
Identifiers: LCCN 2020007830 (print) | LCCN 2020007831 (ebook)
   | ISBN
   9780593135334 (hardcover) | ISBN 9780593135341 (ebook)
Subjects: LCSH: Self-acceptance in women. | Self-actualization (Psychology)
   in women.
Classification: LCC BF575.S37 P47 2020  (print) | LCC BF575.S37  (ebook)
   | DDC 155.3/339—dc23
LC record available at https://lccn.loc.gov/2020007830
LC ebook record available at https://lccn.loc.gov/2020007831

ISBN 978-0-593-13533-4
Ebook ISBN 978-0-593-13534-1

Printed in China

Book design by Danielle Deschenes
Illustrations by Jen B. Peters, Sarah Walsh, Marisol Ortega,
Olivia Herrick, and Danielle Deschenes

Additional credits: page 7 (tiger pouncing) © CSA Images/Getty Images;
page 117 (1960s floral motif) © Galyna_P/Shutterstock

10 9 8 7 6 5 4 3 2 1

First Edition

FOR
ABUELO,

WHO
TAUGHT ME
THERE IS
ALWAYS
**SOMETHING
NEW TO
LEARN.**

# HELLO, AND THANK YOU FOR PICKING UP MY BOOK!

Maybe you're in a bookstore, browsing, and wondering who I am and why you should buy this book. Or perhaps you've already brought it home and you're wondering how to use said book. Well, let's start with who I am. **My name is Ashly Perez. You may recognize me as that girl from BuzzFeed.** I worked there for five-and-a-half years, producing, writing, acting, and directing short-form internet content. Some of my most popular videos included "I Learned How to Dance in 30 Days," in which I mastered a dance routine in order to confront my long-standing body-confidence issues, and "Coming Out," which is a short film about my personal experience coming out as queer. I actually got my start at BuzzFeed as a writer, where I published some of BuzzFeed's earliest viral posts and quizzes. I've been writing my whole life—personally in blogs and journals since I was a kid, and professionally for the past decade. These days, I'm a television writer and artist.

I wrote this book as a response to one of my own issues—something I like to call "phone fatigue." **Most mornings I wake up and find myself immediately reaching for my phone.** Even before my eyes fully open, its blue-light glare is in my face, and the endless scrolling begins, usually through Instagram (for updates on my friends) and Twitter (for updates on the world). It's good to be informed, but my scrolling isn't really satisfying, fulfilling, or inspiring. In fact, most days it leaves me exhausted, sad, or comparing myself to everyone whose life is clearly better than mine—or at least is so in my perception. That's no way to start your day . . . or end your day, or spend any of your day, for that matter. During every break from work, I scroll. In the line at the grocery store, I scroll. When I'm stopped at particularly long red lights, I scroll. I scroll all day until I scroll myself to sleep.

It's not very enriching, but what's the alternative? Enter: *Read This for Inspiration.*

I wrote this book as a remedy for my phone fatigue. I wanted a quick and easy way to take a break from work, munch on a thought-starter, and get back to the business of being a human. I genuinely believe most of us are trying to be better people. We want to treat our bodies better and take time to nourish our souls and our friendships, but it feels impossible to find the time. We relish the thought of starting our days or resetting our minds with a bit of inspiration, but we don't know where to find it.

Sure, there are thousands of inspirational books written by incredible authors, but most of us don't have more than fifteen minutes (if that!) to spare before we start our day. *Read This for Inspiration* is a compilation of the wisdom, encouragement, and enlightenment I've picked up along the way, presented as short, crisp entries—or, as I like to call them, "sparks." No long paragraphs or giant chapters to slog through—instead, I've written disgestible thought-starters you can easily dip into. Scoop them up and take them with you to meditate on throughout your day or as you wind down your night. I've covered all sorts of topics: creativity, belonging, relationships, money, organization, motivation. I've tapped a plethora of sources, including books, music, TED Talks, my social and work experiences, my family. I share lessons, metaphors, and new perspectives that have helped me see my life more clearly and live it more intentionally.

I certainly won't pretend this book is *the* absolute compilation of every bit of inspiration the world has to offer—it's not! But I do hope it serves as a launching point for discovering your own inspiration. You deserve passion in your life. You deserve to be challenged and surprised every day—not just on special occasions. You deserve more than endless scrolling. You deserve quiet moments, introspection, and epiphanies. I hope this book will help you find those signs.

# HOW TO USE THIS BOOK

**1. YOU ARE THE BOSS OF THIS BOOK.** When I was a kid, I loved opening books to random pages, believing that whatever I found was what the universe wanted to show me (unless it wasn't something I wanted to hear—then I would just keep turning until I found something I liked).

You get what I'm saying: Use this book however you like!

On the side of each entry, I've included a tag that notes what sort of topic that entry contains:

body image

<br>

| | | |
|---|---|---|
| body image | science | work |
| self-care | nature | money |
| you do you | growth | food |
| pioneers | self-improvement | hope |
| be bold | motivation | gratitude |
| adventure | do good | grief |
| creativity | family | relaxation |
| words | relationships | don't stress |
| new perspectives | connection | |

You can use these to navigate if you find it helpful. As an extra tool for you, I've included an appendix of the entries, sorted by category, at the end of book. If you find that one day you need a spark of science, for example, this appendix will direct you where to look.

All of the entries are numbered on the bottom or side of the page for easy navigation. Note they are numbered by entry number and not page number.

If you don't need or like these directions, don't follow them! Flip through the book, read it straight through, read it in the morning before you get on your phone, during the work day when you're stressed, or at night right before you go to bed. Keep it in your purse, in your backpack, by your nightstand, or in the top drawer of your work desk. Whatever works for you.

**2. THIS BOOK IS NOT A CHECKLIST.** The intention of *Read This for Inspiration* is *being,* not *doing.* It's meant to help you reflect rather than work. Perhaps the greatest misconception I have been debunking in my own life is that "doing," rather than simply existing, is the thing that makes me valuable. It is my hope that this book helps you make space to *think, reflect, and feel,* rather than overwhelming you with steps to take. Trust that you are valuable for being exactly who you are the moment you picked up this book. Right now. Treat these entries not as a checklist but as a guide.

**3. INSPIRATION IS EVERYWHERE, FOR EVERYONE.** As I mentioned earlier, this is by no means a complete anthology of inspiration. It does not contain the absolute and universal experiences of all humankind; it contains only my own observations and feelings. My hope is not that you are inspired by all the same things as I am, but rather that you learn how to look for and feel ignited by all the things in your life. If this book makes you feel good things, share them—and share that feeling—with others.

**THANK YOU FOR PICKING UP THIS BOOK.** Thank you for reading. Thank you for sharing. I am honored that the universe brought this to your hands in whatever way and for whatever reason it did.

# WE ALL
# HAVE
# SOMETHING
# TO GIVE

The Christmas movie *It's a Wonderful Life* follows a banker named George Bailey, who finds no value in his life until he sees what the world would have been had he never been born. I love this movie—as many others do—and the thing I think about most from it is not any scene in particular. I think of a tiny prop on the set of Bailey's bank: a framed sign that reads ALL YOU CAN TAKE WITH YOU IS THAT WHICH YOU'VE GIVEN AWAY.

What I take from this is that, in the end, we don't have a collection of our own achievements or even of our hard work. We have what we gave to others, whether it was time, energy, money, or our hearts.

## WHAT
## CAN YOU
## GIVE
## TODAY?

ALL YOU CAN
TAKE WITH YOU IS
THAT WHICH
YOU'VE GIVEN AWAY

# Il fau

I've always loved learning new languages, and not simply because of the immense practicality of a new vocabulary. New languages hold within them entirely new ideas and different ways of thinking, communicating, and being in the world.

In French, one of my favorite phrases is *il faut*, which means "I must" or "we must." Although one could argue that the French do have the word *should* in their language (i.e., *devoir*, the verb meaning "to have to"), it is much more common that French speakers will use *il faut*, which translates closer to the English word *must*. *Il faut manger*. We must eat. *Il faut aimer*. We must love.

Must—I love that idea. It leaves no room for uncertainty and insecurity in the way that *should* does.

## Il faut. We must.

What insecurities do you feel in your life today? What do you feel you "should" do, think, or be? *I should call my mom. I should start working out. I should stop being so afraid.* Now, what if all your shoulds were musts? What if you left yourself no choice but to dive in?

## → Il faut. You must.

# HUMBLE

# DOUGHNUTS

Before Oprah Winfrey was Oprah, first name only, she had a hard time getting people to watch the taping of her show in Chicago. No one really wanted to sit in a live audience through some unknown, random woman's daily talk show—they were getting their fill on the genre from Phil Donahue, who at the time had the number one talk show in America. But Oprah (being Oprah) was determined.

Every morning, Oprah would pick up baked goods from her local Dunkin' Donuts and then proceed to stand on the corner of State Street, telling people trudging through the Chicago winter that she had fresh doughnuts, hot coffee, and heat upstairs in her studio. She packed them in one by one until she "became" Oprah—and she didn't need to lure people with doughnuts anymore.

This story reminds us that in chasing our dreams, nothing is above us. Even the biggest superstar of them all comes from humble doughnuts.

## THE
## TWO-MINUTE RULE

One of my former managers at BuzzFeed recommended a book to me called *Getting Things Done: The Art of Stress-Free Productivity* by David Allen. I must admit I don't remember anything from the book except this one thing—and it's changed my life: "Anything you can do in under two minutes, do it now."

That's it. So simple, and yet it's life-changing when applied. When you're stressed, overwhelmed, and paralyzed by how much you have to do or how busy the day-to-day is, focus solely on what you can, right now, do in two minutes or less.

Don't stop to think about it!

■ **DO IT.** ■

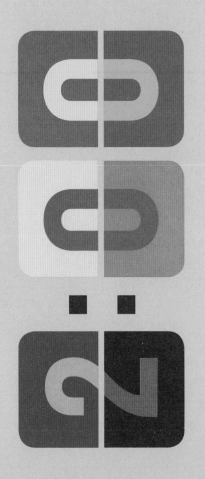

Anything you can do
in under two minutes,
do it now.

motivation / work

In Anne Lamott's famous book on writing, *Bird by Bird*, she recounts a story about her brother, who, at age ten, had a giant school report due on birds that he had been putting off for months until the day before it was due. Completely overwhelmed by the result of his procrastination, he sat paralyzed by the mammoth task ahead of him when their dad sat next to him and simply said, "Bird by bird, buddy."

Like many writers, I think about that book, and specifically that story, often—and not only in reference to writing. The advice is helpful for tackling just about anything life throws at you. Inevitably, no matter how hard you try to avoid it, you will eventually be trapped in a conundrum of your own making, wondering how you got there in the first place. The temptation in that moment is to do pretty much anything other than tackling the actual problem. You'll wonder how you got there. You'll start examining how and why you made decisions. You may even be hit by a very strong urge to clean your entire home or cook enough food for the whole week.

## And yet.

There's only one thing to do. Yup.
Just start—one bird at a time.

## A BEAUTIFUL BROKEN

In the ancient Japanese art of kintsugi, when pottery breaks, it is not automatically thrown away. Instead, the pieces are carefully collected and reassembled into a complete piece, its cracks filled with gold. What was once broken is made beautiful again—even better than before. Literally translated, the word *kintsugi* means "golden joinery."

Sometimes we're too quick to throw away the pieces of our own proverbial pottery. Embarrassed and ashamed of failures, our inclination is to start fresh as soon as possible—to pretend like we never made a mistake in the first place. But in doing so, we lose the beauty that comes from picking ourselves up and making ourselves whole. Perhaps like the kintsugi pieces, what makes us beautiful is our mistakes and the ways in which we've grown to fill in the cracks of our failures.

Before you give up, before you throw away what you've done so far, fill yourself with gold. Proudly display the beautifully veined pottery that proves how far you've come.

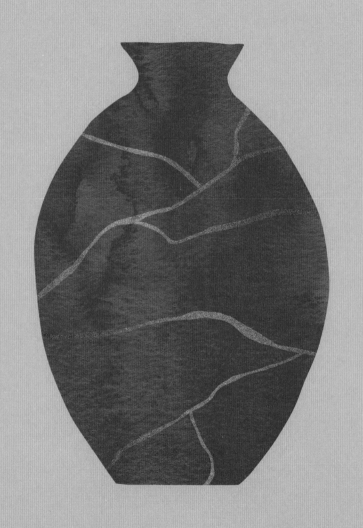

FIGHT THE BIG FIGHTS

In her interview for *Oprah's Master Class*, Barbara Walters's advice to young women was "Fight the big fights, don't fight the little fight. If you don't get all the lines, if you're not where you should be, be the first one in, be the last one out. Do your homework. Choose your battles. Don't whine, and don't be the one who complains about everything. Fight the big fights."

She's right. We are allotted a finite amount of energy each day. The temptation is to give it to anyone who asks, which zaps up the energy we need to accomplish our *own* goals for the day. Don't waste your precious energy on the petty things.

# Fight the big fights.

# Planted

In season one of Netflix's reboot of *Queer Eye*, while planting a garden with a freshly made-over straight man, Bobby Berk, the show's interior designer, said, **"When you're feeling buried, sometimes you're just planted."**

We humans tend to be impatient—we want everything quickly, without having to do any work (or, at least, as little work as possible). We're so desperate for results that we forget we need to give ourselves time to grow. Imagine taking a cake out of the oven halfway through its baking time simply because you want it right now. That cake wouldn't be ready. Same with a garden: If you planted a seed and then went to harvest it the next day, there would be nothing to pick! You, too, need time to develop.

If you're feeling a little buried today, like nothing has changed or you're going nowhere, pause for a second. Look around you—maybe changes are happening, slowly but surely. Maybe you're just planted.

# m a n y waves

The Japanese painter Hokusai was best known for his famous woodblock print that is commonly called "The Great Wave." A feat of Japanese art and style, Hokusai's wave has become one of the most recognizable prints in the world.

But this great wave wasn't Hokusai's only wave. When he painted it in 1831, he was seventy-one years old, but waves were a subject he had been painting his entire life.

In the late 1830s, in a postscript to his work *One Hundred Views of Mount Fuji*, Hokusai wrote, "I have drawn things since I was six. All that

*His first wave, painted at age thirty-three in 1792, was tiny.*

*His second wave, painted at age forty-four in 1803, was a bit bigger.*

I made before the age of sixty-five is not worth counting. At seventy-three I began to understand the true construction of animals, plants, trees, birds, fishes, and insects. At ninety I will enter into the secret of things. At a hundred and ten, everything—every dot, every dash—will live." Hokusai understood that his skills as an artist were ever-evolving—there would always be more to learn.

Perhaps you haven't drawn your great wave yet. Perhaps you're not even sure what your great wave is, and that's okay. Mastery takes time. Like Hokusai, all you can do is continue to paint them.

*His third wave, painted only two years later in 1805, was much closer to what his great wave would eventually become. But Hokusai wouldn't draw his wave again for more than twenty-five years.*

Have you ever tried to clean a greasy pan using only water? Nothing happens. The oil adheres tightly as the water glides right over it, incapable of grabbing on. That's because oil is hydrophobic: It *hates* water.

Enter soap. Soap is weird. Scientifically, it's bipolar: Half of its molecules are hydrophobic (they, too, hate water), and half of them are hydrophilic (they *love* water). Confusing, right? But this split makes soap the go-between, the peacemaker, between water and oil. It bonds water to oil so the oil can slip off the pan.

This morsel of information is my favorite thing I ever learned in any science class. It reminds me that sometimes, despite our strength and our best efforts, we need a little help. We need a friend who has something we don't have ourselves. Needing help doesn't make us weak (or weaker), it makes us human.

Who's your soap? Who helps you when you can't seem to help yourself? And whose soap might you be?

A LITTLE CONTEXT

This is a picture of Earth taken by Voyager 1 on February 14, 1990, as it reached the outer bounds of our solar system. From 4 billion miles away, we are just a tiny dot hidden in the midst of scattered light rays.

Carl Sagan said of astronomy in his book *Pale Blue Dot*, "It's a humbling and character-building experience." Of this image, he said, "There is perhaps no better demonstration of the folly of human conceits than this distant image of our tiny world." Indeed, this picture is a reminder of our own insignificance in this ever-expanding universe, but that doesn't depress me. Rather, I find comfort in the humility of knowing we are in some ways unimportant—just specks of dust floating in a sunbeam. With this perspective, we can forget all the stresses that occupy our minds and overtake us, remembering that everything that will ever come to be is just a tiny dot. A dot of peace in the context of our existence.

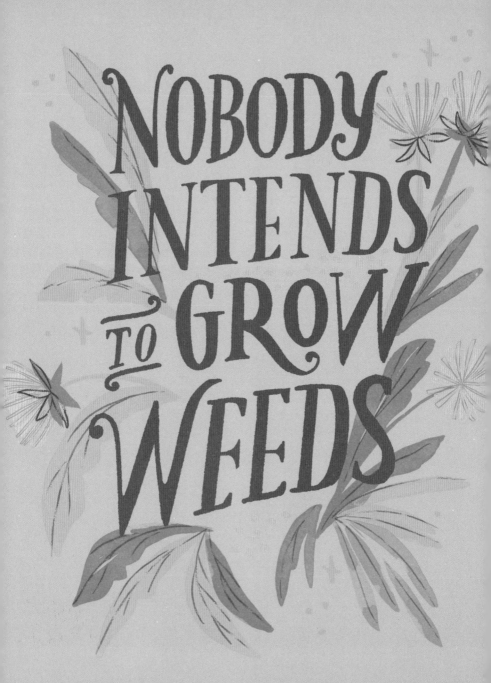

Have you ever seen a garden without any weeds? No. None of us *intends* to grow weeds when we plant our gardens. But inevitably they appear. However, flowers don't stop blooming because weeds appear. Bees don't stop pollinating. Plants don't stop exchanging carbon for oxygen.

We don't cease to be a garden because one day we find ourselves surrounded by weeds. Simply pick out your weeds and keep growing strong.

Create,

motivation

## THE GIFT OF

# MOMENTUM

For humans, change is difficult. So is confronting our demons. We all practice patterns and reactions that have, over time, crystallized into habits that at some point became no longer helpful to us. My best friend, Catherine, put it to me this way: "I realize there are all these roadblocks in my life. I can either start to move them out of my way and change, or I can keep ramming into them and go nowhere."

How do you start moving roadblocks you've grown comfortable working around, though? How do you change patterns you've developed over a lifetime? The answer is to give yourself momentum.

Physics tells us that an object in motion tends to stay in motion, while an object at rest tends to stay at rest. If you want to change, start by taking one step. Put yourself in motion. Give yourself the gift of momentum. Only then will you start moving your roadblocks.

Take your space

Have you ever noticed how rebellious
    flowers are?

Growing where they shouldn't be.
In between cracks in the asphalt, on the
    sides of roads.

They take their space, even when the
    world has not made room for them.

FILL
YOURSELF
UP
FIRST

Perhaps the most helpful tip I've learned about helping others and giving myself to others came from a simple analogy about a cup, a pitcher, and a bowl.

You are the cup, the pitcher is what you have to give, and the bowl is those who need what you are giving.

If you use the cup to draw water from the pitcher in order to pour it into the bowl, there will always be a moment between pours in which the cup is completely empty. But if you put the cup inside the bowl and pour the water from the pitcher into the cup, then eventually it will overflow into the surrounding bowl. You will never be empty, even when you are giving.

If you find yourself in a situation of helping people in any way, you may be tempted to give your all at the expense of yourself. Whether you're the go-to friend for talking through an emotionally difficult time, a mom fulfilling your children's needs, or a boss attempting to do right by your employees, you cannot always give to others before you give to yourself.

Find a moment or two for yourself today. Fill up your cup. Then give freely of yourself.

**YOU'VE GOT TIME**

Lucille Ball was a master of comedy—the doyenne. Almost everyone has seen at least one episode of *I Love Lucy* at some point in their life. To this day, it remains one of the most popular and successful television shows of all time.

But before *I Love Lucy* premiered, Lucille Ball was on the verge of quitting acting: a washed-up, C-list, blonde wannabe movie star who still hadn't made her mark on Hollywood after twenty-plus years in the business. Everyone had already given up on her. Everyone thought she had missed her shot at stardom. That is, everyone except Lucille herself.

Lucille Ball was forty years old when the first episode of *I Love Lucy* premiered on CBS. This reminds me that I've got time—and so do you.

If you're worried that you're never going to make it, that you've used up all your chances, and you think maybe you should just give up, remember Lucy.

## FEEL YOUR FEELINGS

One of the most profoundly simple lessons I've learned is that we are supposed to feel our feelings. It sounds elementary to have to say it, but I wonder how many of us try to do exactly the opposite.

When we're happy, we might feel frivolous and unproductive. When we're sad, the unrelenting unpleasantness is uncomfortable. So we often banish extreme feelings of joy or sadness. But that's not what feelings are for! They aren't meant to be flashes we acknowledge and then quickly dispel. They are meant to be felt for exactly as long as the feeling stays around.

A proverb from the thirteenth-century Persian poet Rumi exemplifies this sentiment well.

*I said: What about my heart?*
*He said: Tell me what you hold inside it?*
*I said: Pain and sorrow.*
*He said: Stay with it. The wound is the place where the*
*Light enters you.*

If you finally get the good news you've been waiting for, don't stop the elation by downplaying your achievement. Jump around the room, do a silly dance, call your best friend to celebrate. If you experience a loss, don't minimize your hurt. Listen to sad songs, cry, write stream-of-consciousness journal entries. If you're angry, scream. Anxiety, frustration, boredom—*feel* them. Emotions are gifts, tiny moments to connect with yourself. And maybe, just maybe, if you stay with your feelings, a little light will find space to enter.

# IF YOU'RE LOST:

Many of us experience a time in our lives when we feel lost. Maybe you went through a breakup, lost a job, or experienced the death of a loved one. You are on a precipice, and now the anxiety of uncertainty has settled in.

It was during a time like this in my own life, after I had graduated from college and had no job prospects, that I discovered some advice that broadcast journalist Diane Sawyer's father had given her when she was stuck in the same boat of not knowing which way to proceed. He said:

DO WHAT YOU LOVE.

DO IT IN THE MOST
EXCITING PLACE POSSIBLE.

MAKE SURE IT HELPS
PEOPLE.

**THAT'S IT. AND IT'S EVERGREEN:** Even though I'm past that terrifying moment of uncertainty, I've found that this advice helps me whenever I'm at a crossroads or given an opportunity to reassess a situation.

Notions of beauty in Japan and in the Western world are wholly different. Western aesthetics prioritize clean lines, symmetry, and perfection. The Japanese aesthetic known as wabi-sabi values the ordinary, imperfection, and purposeful ruggedness.

*Wabi-sabi* cannot be precisely translated into English. This word and others like it—*joie de vivre* in French, *duende* in Spanish—seem to embody a way of life more than anything else. Originally derived from Zen Buddhism, wabi-sabi is the concept that imperfection and age are not only acceptable, they are what makes something beautiful. A wooden desk covered in scratches, nicks, and water rings is not in need of repair; it is beautiful *because* of its wear.

In a way, wabi-sabi is a direct contradiction to Western consumerism, because it values objects, buildings, plates, and people not for their perfection or newness but for their wisdom, age, and experience of living. In it lies a freedom that so often escapes Western culture and our ongoing filtering of life until it's what we deem perfect. There is freedom in knowing of a different way to live. If you, like me, are tired of the pressure to be perfect, to fix your flaws, to hide your imperfections, then join me today in the wabi-sabi that is life.

# WABI-

# SABI

Savor it

TAKE A SIP
Practice mindfulness

Have you ever had a perfectly foamy latte, or a piping-hot pot of tea, or any other sort of delicious drink in front of you—ready for consumption—only to find that the next time you look down, you've already finished it? An entire beverage is gone without your having enjoyed it—without mindfulness.

Distilled, mindfulness is about savoring the moment you're in. The root of the word *savor* comes from the Latin *sapere*, which means "to taste." Savoring is as simple as tasting—active awareness of the moment your coffee or tea hits your tongue. What does it taste like? Can you feel it traveling down your throat? Is it warming? Refreshing? Are you enjoying it?

## Take a sip.
## Practice mindfulness.
## Savor it.

# THREE LESSONS I'VE LEARNED FROM CILANTRO

NOT EVERYBODY IS GOING TO LIKE YOU, AND THAT'S OKAY. Some people will love you; some people won't be able to stand you. You are what you are.

THE GOOD STUFF ISN'T JUST THE PRETTY STUFF. A great deal of cilantro's flavor comes from its stems, not just its pretty leaves. Looks aren't everything.

YOU DON'T HAVE TO BE SALT TO ADD FLAVOR.

Salty attitudes get a lot of attention, but you don't have to act that way. You can be like an aromatic and be generous with your flavor without being overpowering.

keep only good energy

Do a simple check of the people around you, and of the things you read, watch, and consume. Do they give you energy? Or do they take it from you?

If they don't give you energy, pull away. You don't have room for anything that sucks your energy. Your energy needs to be bolstered. Don't settle for anything less.

## YOUR MISTAKES WILL MAKE YOU BETTER

There's a story in one of my favorite books, *Art & Fear*, by David Bayles and Ted Orland, that describes a class of art students who were split into two groups. Group 1 would have to make only one pot the entire time they were in their pottery class. If the pot was perfect, they would get an A. Group 2 would be graded on the number of pots they made throughout the semester: Make fifty pots to get an A, forty pots to get a B, and so on. Guess who did better? That's right: Group 2.

Group 1 was so obsessed with getting its one pot exactly right that they feared making every single choice. *What if a decision was wrong?* They toiled and toiled, and they worried and worried, and they ended up making nothing, because they had learned nothing. The one pot was imbued with too much pressure.

Group 2, on the other hand, learned something new with every pot they formed. By pot number 50, they were able to make the perfect pot, because they had learned from failures along the way. Pot 2 taught them not to add too much water to the clay. Pot 29's lesson was not making their pot too thin. Pot 38 taught them that even a perfect pot can be destroyed by the wrong glaze. This went on until, by pot 50, they had learned it all.

If you're a creative person and you have a project you desperately want to perfect, embrace that you have more than one opportunity to try. Give yourself over to the process and learn as you go. After you've made all the mistakes, you might just learn how to make the perfect pot.

growth / work / creativity

THE URGE TO SHOP

I have always been an impulsive person, and therefore an impulsive shopper. This habit has led to a cycle of constant buying and purging that has left my house full of clutter and me with the unsettling feeling of not being in control. I made many attempts to stop this pattern through sheer willpower and meticulous tracking. None of it worked.

Now, whenever I feel the urge to make a purchase, I write down what I want to buy and why I want to buy it. Why do I want to go out and buy iced coffee even though I have a perfect batch of cold brew sitting in my refrigerator? Because I want to feel productive. Because when I'm sitting at home between freelance gigs, I feel purposeless. The act of acquiring the coffee gives me an instant ping of relief—until the feeling returns. *I want to buy iced coffee to feel like I am doing something.*

Asking yourself why you are buying something is an excellent way to reveal your fears and avoidances. I found that almost every purchase I wanted to make was aimed at masking my insecurities.

Write down the what and the why of your shopping urges. See what you find—and what you actually need.

*Write down the what and why of your shopping urges.*

**SEE WHAT YOU FIND—
AND WHAT YOU
ACTUALLY NEED.**

THE TERM "MAGIC HOUR" REFERS TO THE TIME JUST BEFORE SUNRISE OR RIGHT AFTER SUNSET WHEN THE SUN IS NO LONGER VISIBLE IN THE SKY, BUT ITS LIGHT STILL LINGERS. CINEMATOGRAPHERS

BEAUTIFUL TIME TO MAKE FILMS, I THINK MAGIC HOUR IS ALSO THE MOST BEAUTIFUL TIME TO THINK AND BE INSPIRED. IT'S DURING MAGIC HOUR THAT I DO MOST OF MY WRITING. FOR MOST

OF US, MAGIC HOUR IS DURING THE TIME DIRECTLY BEFORE AND AFTER WORK

WE START THE WHOLE MAD RUSH OVER AGAIN, WE LITERALLY MISS

THE MAGIC. CHOOSE WONDER TODAY: LOOK UP THE TIME OF THE SUNSET OR SUNRISE, POP

OUTSIDE, AND WATCH THE MAGIC. ★

CALL IT "MAGIC HOUR" BECAUSE EVERYTHING IS SO BEAUTIFULLY, EVENLY, AND DIFFUSELY LIT

(DEPENDING ON THE TIME OF YEAR). AND YET MOST OF US NEVER EXPERIENCE IT—

THAT IT CREATES AN AURA OF, WELL, MAGIC ON FILM. ASIDE FROM BEING THE MOST BEAUTIFUL TIME TO MAKE FILMS,

WE ARE TOO BUSY EITHER PREPARING FOR WORK OR HURRIEDLY TRYING TO GET HOME, FEED OURSELVES,

MAGIC HOUR

AND SQUEEZE A FEW HOURS OF RELAXATION INTO THE END OF OUR DAY BEFORE

I THINK THAT IT CREATES AN AURA OF, WELL, MAGIC ON FILM, ASIDE FROM BEING THE MOST

## EASY GRATI- TUDE

Perhaps the most effective way to be happier is to be grateful for what we already have. I know, I know. But honestly? It's a hell of a lot easier than changing everything about yourself and constantly striving to be a new, better you.

To help you out, here are some quick things you can do today, for free, to start practicing gratitude.

**CHANGE THE LOCKSCREEN ON YOUR PHONE TO A PICTURE OF THE BEST THING THAT HAPPENED TO YOU THIS WEEK.** Maybe it was a pretty flower, a selfie with a friend you haven't seen in a while, or a photo of your dog sleeping. Whatever it is, it's going to make you smile every time you see it. Make a habit of changing this picture every week to help you remember there's always something new to be grateful for.

**WRITE DOWN THREE THINGS YOU WERE GRATEFUL FOR TODAY.** Less traffic? A yummy breakfast? The song you were listening to ending just as you arrived at your destination?

**TEXT SOMEONE YOU HAVEN'T SEEN IN A LITTLE WHILE AND THANK THEM FOR A MEMORY YOU HAVE TOGETHER.** It's easy to forget we have friends and experiences all over the place. You can call upon them any time.

## SAFE AND BORED

"A ship in harbor is safe, but that is not what ships are built for." Like all the best inspiration, I originally found this quote on a magnet.

A number of famous people throughout history have drawn inspiration from these words, including President Theodore Roosevelt, who (among other things) added more than 200 million acres of land to the American national parks, and Rear Admiral Grace Hopper, a trailblazer in computer programming and software development—both mavericks in their own right. Both people who spent their lives outside of a safe harbor. Both people who understood what ships were built for. *Yeah, you're safe, but are you doing what you're supposed to be doing?* Or, as I like to put it: You're safe, but are you bored? Are you dreaming of what your life would be like on the open seas?

What is it that you're
not doing today?
Why haven't you started
doing it yet?
Could you try today?

# DON'T WAIT, START

On the press tour for the movie *Wine Country*, her directorial debut, Netflix Film asked Amy Poehler about her advice to other young female filmmakers. She said, "Do it even if you don't think you're ready . . . A lot of young women wait until they think they're really, really ready for something. And I've worked with a lot of guys who aren't ready for what they're doing."

What's the point in waiting until you're perfect at something to start it? You are capable enough right now. Listen to Amy. Don't wait.

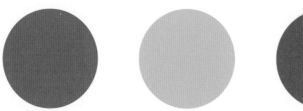

**EVERY-THING IS COPY**

Nora Ephron is perhaps best known as the queen of rom-coms. She wrote or directed some of the most iconic movies of the '80s, '90s, and 2000s: *Heartburn, When Harry Met Sally, Sleepless in Seattle, You've Got Mail, Julie & Julia.* But before she was a screenwriter, she was a journalist, essayist, and columnist. She was a voice for women in an era when women were just starting to find their voices in media and in the workplace.

My favorite thing Nora Ephron ever said was "Everything is copy." Or, actually, I suppose it was something her mother, who was also a writer, said to her. According to Ephron's sons, these words mean that every experience you have—good, bad, hilarious, traumatic, or otherwise—can be used later on in your life to tell a story. Experiences become words. It's all copy.

Today, don't dwell on the details or the small embarrassments. File them away to entertain or teach someone else later.

# THE IN-BETWEEN SPACES

I never quite fit into just one box—literally. I am Cuban, Korean, and Filipino. I'm queer, I grew up with immigrant parents, and I dabbled in four different college majors before I landed on one (and it was one that has absolutely nothing to do with my work now). For most of my life, not belonging to a single group gave me a great deal of anxiety. I so badly longed to be a straight, white, blonde girl who could move through the world as easily as a table knife through warm butter.

To speak plainly: I don't feel that way anymore. I can't pinpoint the exact moment at which I began accepting and loving myself for who I am, but the change mostly has to do with being comfortable occupying the in-between spaces.

I first heard that term—the in-between spaces—in a sociology class, referencing the lesbian Chicana artists who didn't seem to fit into any one group. They claimed to occupy the in-between spaces—the spaces between the spaces, the centers of the Venn diagrams. Just knowing that these women who also felt othered existed helped me feel understood. Until then, I didn't know there was a space between the spaces—a space for me.

Whoever you are, you have multiplicities within you. Take pride in them, in accepting every bit of who you are, and in celebrating it.

Today, I lead with the qualities that I used to hide behind. I proudly declare that my parents weren't born here, that I am as much the daughter of immigrants as I am American, and that I am queer. When we step into who we really are, we can begin to clear a path for others to do the same. Celebrate yourself today. Take up the in-between spaces, because someone else out there needs you to be you.

# A TINY TUGBOAT

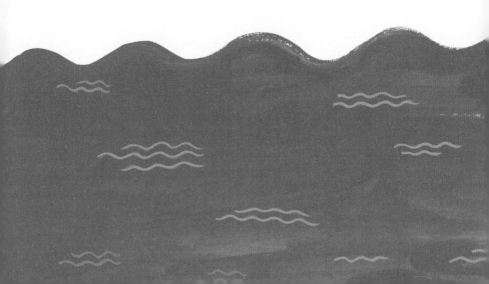

can pull a gigantic ship all on its own.

# DON'T

UNDERESTIMATE YOUR POWER JUST BECAUSE YOU ARE SEEMINGLY SMALLER THAN THE GIANTS AROUND YOU.

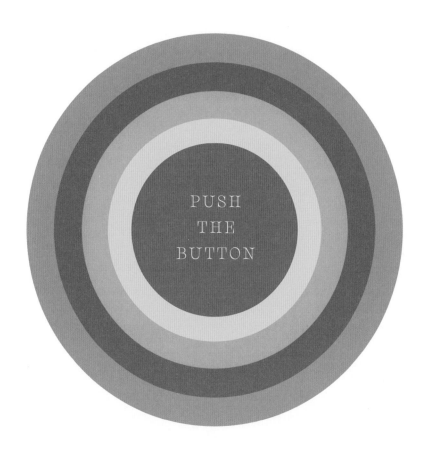

PUSH
THE
BUTTON

In 1962, Carol Burnett signed a ten-year contract with CBS that required her to do one comedy special per year, as well as a few guest spots on the network's other shows. But one of the deal's terms was especially interesting: If, during its first five years, Burnett wanted to do a variety show, the network would be obligated to air thirty one-hour episodes, no questions asked. All she had to do was "push the button," and they would have to execute.

Five days before the end of that five-year period, Burnett pushed the button. She called up one of CBS's vice presidents. He told her, "Comedy, variety . . . Carol, it's a man's game. It's just not for you gals." He offered her a sitcom instead, called *Here's Agnes*. But Carol wanted a variety show, and CBS had no choice but to give it to her.

*The Carol Burnett Show* debuted in 1967, the first variety hour to be hosted by a woman. It ran for eleven years and won twenty-five Emmy awards. Carol Burnett now has a lifetime achievement award *named after her* at the Golden Globes.

If there's a button and you want to push it, don't let anyone stop you.

### DON'T SKIP THE MONTAGE

You know the feeling you get when you watch the *Rocky II* training montage? The famous one where Rocky prepares for his big fight and races up the steps in front of the Philadelphia Museum of Art. It's a feeling of pure elation. *He did it! Nothing can stop him! Go, Rocky!*

We all love to watch it, but rarely do we want to climb those steps ourselves. Without the montage, there is no movie, though—the struggle is what makes victory so sweet. Like Rocky, you have a dream, a "big fight" to win. Don't do yourself the disservice of cutting out your montage. Enjoy the sweat and relish your win.

I'm sure you've heard the phrase "Curiosity killed the cat," but you may not have heard the rest of the adage: "Curiosity killed the cat, but satisfaction brought it back."

*you do you*

*be curious*

*find out*

*feel satisfied*

Whenever I would go to my grandparents' house in Redlands, California, I'd spend the majority of my time with my abuelo in the living room, learning about our family history. He'd pull out all the photo albums, spread them over the dining room table, and we'd dive in.

One day, I was reciting our family lineage back to my abuelo, my brain nearing its capacity to learn, when I realized I hadn't seen my abuela in a few hours. I signaled that I wanted to take a break, and I went in search of her. After just a few minutes, I found her sitting outside on the porch. She had been there for hours.

I sat in the chair next to her, expecting her to turn to me and start talking, asking me the kinds of prodding questions that grandparents love to ask. But she didn't move. She continued looking out onto the street, completely peaceful and comfortable in her silence.

Continued on next page

# MIRANDO.

# LOOKING.

This lack of conversation and of eye contact gave me immense anxiety. I wasn't quite sure what we were "doing" out there. I took out my phone, took a few pictures, and scrolled through a few apps, until I quickly ran out of things to do. Finally, I turned to her and asked, *"Abuela, que estas haciendo?"* What are you doing? She turned to me and smiled. *"Mirando."* Looking.

When I turned back to take in what she had been looking at, my view was completely different. I saw birds hopping from tree to tree, cars gently passing every few minutes. I heard the fountain bubbling over in front of the garden. Even the noisy racket of the lawn mower next door was somehow calming. With one simple word, my abuela had freed me from doing and challenged me to be an observer, welcoming me into the center of that very place and time.

Sometimes, when I'm overwhelmed, I think back to that afternoon. I close my eyes and transport myself to that porch where my job is not to do, but rather to look. Close your eyes and join us on the porch.

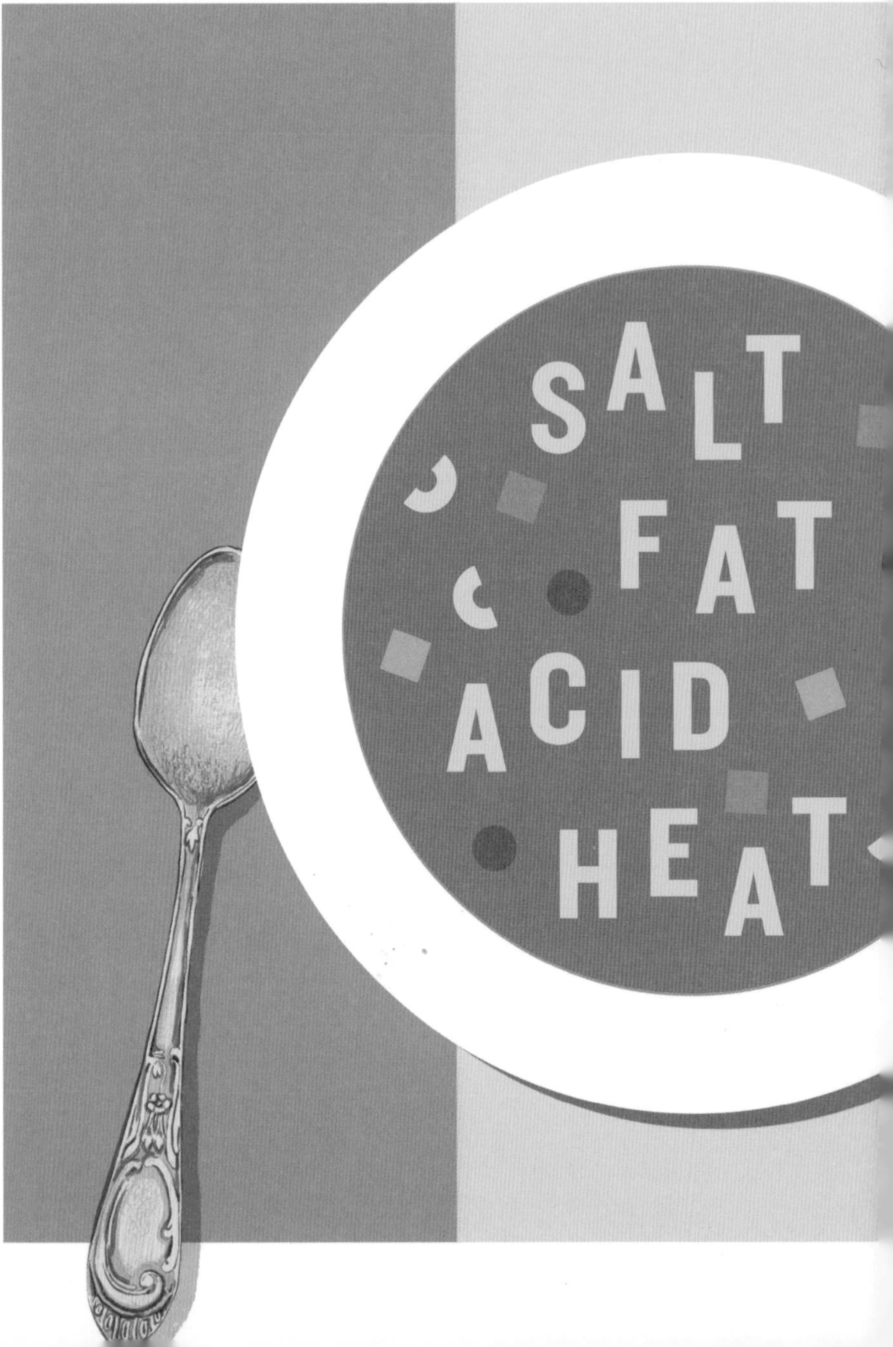
SALT
FAT
ACID
HEAT

Samin Nosrat's Netflix docu-series *Salt Fat Acid Heat*, based on her debut cookbook of the same name, comforts me. Salt, fat, acid, and heat are the four pillars on which all good cooking stand.

Aside from the utter charm of Nosrat, it's this premise that keeps bringing me back. The idea that, despite the hundreds of thousands of dishes eaten all around the world in hundreds of different countries, the building blocks of a great dish remain the same. And they're simple! There are only four of them.

This discovery of the universal soothes me. We all look at the same moon at night; we all learn the same math at school. While the flavors might change, the components of good food remain the same. Maybe we're sharing more meals together than we thought.

LOVE
WHAT
YOU
LOVE

Before he was a famed television personality, Mister Rogers had many other lives. First, he studied in the seminary to become a minister. Then, interested in the upcoming medium of television, he took a job at a public television station. While working there, he was part of a group of researchers at the forefront of childhood development studies.

On their own, these disparate interests wouldn't seem to belong to one individual. But this precise combination of interests made Mister Rogers perfect for the job of children's TV show host—they made him the only person who could have done the job so well, or at least who could have done the job exactly as he did it.

Some days, you might feel like your own version of Mister Rogers, caught in a storm of disparate interests that don't quite seem to gel. Maybe you've decided you should abandon some of your passions in favor of getting serious about one. But if you limit yourself, you lose your greatest potential of all: the potential to bring an entirely unique set of interests to the world.

Follow all of your passions, even—and especially—the ones that don't outwardly make sense. Love what you love; it's the combination of all the things you care about that makes you what the world needs. And, as Mister Rogers said at the end of each episode of his show, "I like you as you are."

it

is

free

do good

to

be

kind

## HEALING WHAT'S UNDER-NEATH

Scabs are not pretty. They are actually quite gross, practically by definition, but what scabs do is pretty amazing. When your skin breaks, whether it's a cut, a scrape, or anything else, you're immediately vulnerable—in pain, probably, but also susceptible to dirt, grime, and bacteria from the world around you. But big or small, your cut will soon start to form a scab. A scab protects you and, quite literally, draws your separated skin back together. A scab offers a safe way for your body to heal what's under the surface.

Sometimes something ugly and hard needs to cover what's going on inside, providing an extra layer of protection. Maybe you're going through a lot right now. Maybe it feels like too much to handle, and maybe you need a tiny break from all the bad trying to get into your wound. It's okay to have a scab. It's okay to put up a temporary barrier between the world and your troubles while you heal. Change isn't always easy or pretty. Don't dismay; soon you'll be on the other side of the hard stuff, with a layer of fresh skin to start over.

# DARK MATTER

We have no idea what a full 95 percent of the universe is made up of. If you don't have it all figured out quite yet, you're probably good.

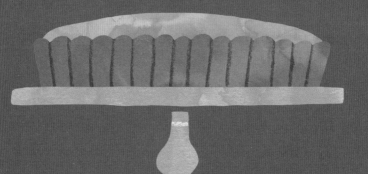

LiFE'S
TOO ShORt

NOt TO
EAt TARt.

Madame Langford was the most delightfully kooky French professor I had in college. In truth, she rarely taught us French, but she did teach me more about *Frenchness* (and living in general) than any other teacher in my life.

"In France, an affair is called *une aventure*, because that's all it is: a quick adventure."

*"Le professeur n'est jamais en retard."* The professor is never late. (It's worth noting that Madame Langford strolled into class fifteen minutes late almost every day.)

"Women are so powerful, we only have to puff our lips, expel a bit of air, and walk away to end an argument, taking all the power from a man."

My favorite story was about when Madame Langford was a young model in France. Hungry for lunch after finishing a job, she found a row of delicious, perfectly cooked shrimp tarts just waiting to be enjoyed. "Mademoiselle, perhaps you should eat *une petite salade*. You are getting a bit too big," the modeling director told her as she reached for one.

"I quit," Madame Langford pointedly replied. "Life is too short not to eat tart."

Sure, she was a little bit eccentric, but perhaps she was a genius as well.

## STAY IN YOUR LANE

One of my favorite poems is "Desiderata" by Max Ehrmann, at least in part for the way it makes me think new things upon each rereading. In it, a passage near the beginning goes like this:

*If you compare yourself with others,*
*you may become vain and bitter;*
*for always there will be greater and lesser persons*
*than yourself.*
*Enjoy your achievements as well as your plans.*

Comparison will kill you, because no matter who you are, someone will always be better than you, and someone else worse. It is both maddening and freeing to acknowledge this truth.

The best advice I've ever received came from my friend Quinta, who first showed me "Desiderata." I was feeling insecure about my job and my place at work, because Quinta, one of my closest friends and coworkers, had just been promoted and I wasn't. She told me to "stay in my lane." She said, "I'm in my lane, and you're in yours. Neither lane is better than the other."

We all have our own thing. Her success didn't mean I wouldn't also have success one day—it just meant we were on different paths. Staying in my lane has provided me with tremendous peace, as I now know that my lane, my path, is my own and has nothing to do with anyone else's. Whether you listen to Max Ehrmann or to Quinta, remember that you are in competition with no one but yourself.

**PICK A LETTER** When I was in college and feeling particularly bored or restless, I would call up a friend, ask if they were free, and then tell them to meet me in the parking lot in ten minutes.

"Pick a letter." I would say, and I was always met with a perplexed "What???" in response.

"Pick a letter. Any letter."

"All right . . . R."

Then we'd get in the car, and we'd be off. We'd get on the highway and drive until we found an exit that started with the letter R, and from there, we'd drive until we found a restaurant we wanted to try—always somewhere new. Not only would I get an adventure out of this exercise, I'd always learn something new about my friend during the ride, too.

Adding variety to your everyday life is the easiest way to get yourself out of a rut. It shakes off the feeling of restlessness that has probably been collecting in your soul. The more shocking the variety, the bigger the shake-up, so challenge yourself to change in the most creative way possible. Instead of adding a different creamer to your coffee, grab a friend and play my letter game. Just know that if they pick X, you might be driving for a while.

When I let my apartment get dirty, I let it get all the way dirty. Inevitably, eventually, I come to a moment when I suddenly realize I have been living in an absolute pigsty and must immediately clean everything in sight. I begin moving bits and bobs off every surface: a pair of socks under the coffee table, kitchen scissors that have migrated to the entry-way table, every pair of pants I've worn that week left exactly where I took them off. I clean like this for hours, but I don't see any change. Nothing is more frustrating than seeing no progress after working for hours on end.

It's then that I remember that picking up a little bit from every-where never helps. And so I change tacks from focusing on bits and bobs to going surface by surface.

I completely clear off the chair in my room, then the top of my desk, then all the books strewn across my bed, until finally order begins to emerge around me.

The finance world calls this one-surface-at-a-time approach the "snowball theory," and financial advisers use it to help people get out of debt. If you have seven credit cards that are maxed out and rapidly collecting interest, you'll never get out of debt by paying the minimum monthly payment on all seven of them. Snowball theory targets the smallest debt first by paying it off aggressively. Of course, you have to continue to pay the monthly minimums on your other cards, but at least you see measurable progress. You don't suddenly have more money, but by seeing this progress, you create your own forward momentum, inciting a snowball effect.

Whether it's a dirty room, debt, or any other task you've been letting build up, know that you can't start everywhere all at once. Pick a single surface, start your snowball, and give yourself the push you need.

**SUCCESS IS A SNOWBALL**

The singer and songwriter Lizzo released the single "Truth Hurts" in September 2017. It didn't become a number one hit until September 2019. Work, ideas, and art can be good before they've been validated. Sometimes it takes people a while to realize someone's greatness.

We slept on Lizzo for two years—no doubt, we're definitely sleeping on someone else who is also 100 percent that bitch right now. Whoever you are, keep hustlin'. Make Lizzo proud; we'll find you.

Progress is
a horseshoe

If you've ever tried to create anything, you know it's frustrating. And I do mean anything: writing a poem, baking a cake, even painting a mug at one of those mug-painting places.

The problem with creating is that you have this idea in your head—and while it's in your head, it's perfect. A lovely little thing to hold in your mind's eye! But then comes the trying. You start making the perfect thing, and suddenly it's not what you'd imagined. The discrepancy could range from the thing being really quite bad to being just a touch off.

Ira Glass, the noted NPR personality, calls this phenomenon "the gap." The gap between your taste and your abilities. Yes, of course you have good taste. You know what you want to make, but in the actual making of it, you find that you fall short. And because it's not what

you'd expected, you stop. Why would you keep going? It's not what you wanted to make!

But if you don't keep going, you'll never get closer to making the thing that was in your mind.

My watercolor teacher had a way around the gap. She said, "Making things is not a straight line, it's more like a horseshoe." You start off at one point, and before you get back to where you were, it gets a whole lot worse. You dip down to the lowest part of the horseshoe, certain you'll never be able to claw your way back up. But you do, and you do, and then, eventually, you're back to where you started.

So, if you feel like you're in the gap, just keep going until you're back to the top of the horseshoe.

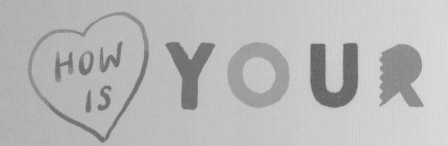

HOW IS YOUR

I try to go home to San Diego whenever I can. As the daughter of immigrants who are obsessed with family, I have come to understand that your parents will always want to see you. One weekend, when I was twenty-four and experiencing a minor heartbreak, I went down to clear my head of Los Angeles and the crush who had rejected me.

The weekend passed quietly, consisting mostly of taking naps, eating home-cooked meals, and lounging in the family room. And then, on my final day, as we were walking along the bay in Coronado, my mom asked me a question that reminded me why I will always need home, no matter how old I am. "How's your heart?" she said matter-of-factly. I could tell she had been dying to ask me all weekend, but she wanted it to be a private

# HEA**R**T?

moment shared between the two of us instead of a family discussion. I appreciated this; my mom always knows how and when to bring up a sensitive subject.

I was about to answer with a rote "I'm okay" when I realized she didn't ask me, "How are you?" She specifically asked, "How's your heart?" There's a world of difference. She didn't care what I'd been watching on Netflix or what I'd Instagrammed that day. In that moment, I understood: Home really is where the heart is. Even when you're away, home wonders how your heart is doing.

Who is your home? Who asks about your heart? It doesn't have to be a biological parent, by the way. Home comes in many forms. Who brings you back when you've drifted away? Call home.

KOMOREBI

Did you know there is a Japanese word for the way the light filters through the leaves? *Komorebi.* That is how beautiful the world we live in can be: so beautiful that an entire, individual, unique word is required for this tiny, specific, beautiful thing.

Remember that one of the joys of your life can be that you get to observe the stunning way in which the sunlight shines through the leaves.

suspected to have been created by the impact of giant asteroids crashing.

I often become overwhelmed by all that needs to be done to improve our world, and how there never seems to be enough time, money, or energy to make a real difference. But then I think about Jupiter—a planet literally taking the blow when we can't handle the impact—and I realize that helping can be as simple as being an advocate: offering my voice, my privilege, or my influence to someone who needs my help.

How can you be Jupiter in your own solar system? Take stock of the ways in which your gravity may be able to lessen a blow to someone else.

# DO THE DAMN THING!

Sometimes I get overwhelmed by the amount of stuff I have. I look around and feel stressed out by the lack of available physical space.

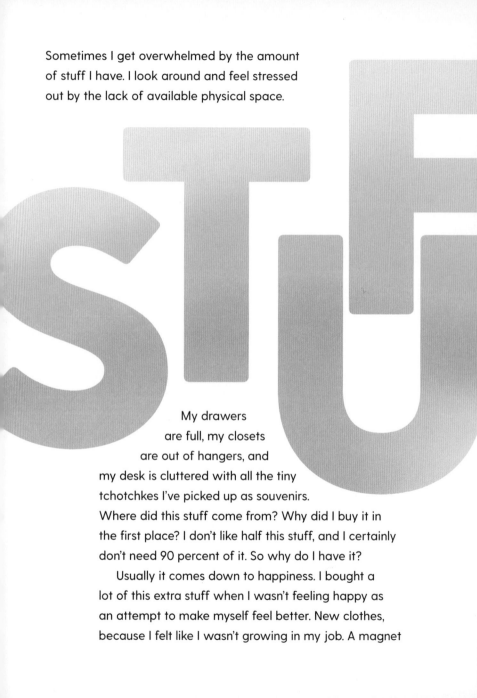

My drawers are full, my closets are out of hangers, and my desk is cluttered with all the tiny tchotchkes I've picked up as souvenirs. Where did this stuff come from? Why did I buy it in the first place? I don't like half this stuff, and I certainly don't need 90 percent of it. So why do I have it?

Usually it comes down to happiness. I bought a lot of this extra stuff when I wasn't feeling happy as an attempt to make myself feel better. New clothes, because I felt like I wasn't growing in my job. A magnet with an inspiring quote, because it said something I aspired to practice. Another pair of gym shoes, because I wasn't happy with my physical appearance. All bought in a moment of impulse, and all abandoned when my reality didn't change. In all these cases, I had hoped a thing would be a quick fix for the real problems in my life. Stuff can never do that. Stuff is the physical manifestation of mental clutter.

We are socialized to be consumers—a fact that didn't dawn on me until I realized how wild it is that we advertise to children, prepping them from childhood to be good shoppers. But there are plenty of other ways to soothe the soul.

**You are not what you buy.** You are not your shoes, your books, or your brands. You are a human being whose survival for most of history has been dependent on social connection. You are not hardwired for stuff, for things, for excess. You are hardwired for sunrises, family, trees, friends, laughter, dancing, flowers, community, and the gentle chirp of the crickets.

**WHAT IF YOU DON'T BUY ANYTHING TODAY?**

Instead, take stock of how you feel and what might actually celebrate or soothe that emotion.

# THE SUN IS ALWAYS SHINING

Visualization is a common practice within meditation. As the name suggests, you visualize different ideas or concepts in order to help alleviate stress or anxiety. My favorite visualization, perhaps, is a calm and quiet forest. I'll take you there.

There is hardly any noise except for the tiny rustle of leaves and the gentle trickle of a small stream somewhere out of sight. You are comfortably seated on a soft bed of grass, and shining down on you is a single sunbeam.

You breathe with awareness as the sunbeam spreads over your whole body. You feel it travel from the top of your head, across your chest and arms, down your stomach and your legs, until finally, it warms even the bottoms of your feet. Breathe in and out, in and out, absorbing the sunbeam. Take a break to revisit this forest and soak up this sunbeam's warmth anytime you need to.

HATERS AREN'T MAKERS

There's a lot of talk about "haters"—people who seem to only know how to criticize. But there's even more talk about what to do about those haters. *Shake it off. Block out the haters. F*ck the haters.* These responses are all reasonable, given the endless barrage of criticism and negativity coming from said haters.

But blocking out the haters can be dangerous. Where do we draw the line between true hatred and constructive criticism? Can we really just block out everything we don't want to hear? How can we tell the difference?

Brené Brown, the famous author, researcher, and speaker on shame and vulnerability, has a succinct answer to these questions. She says in her Netflix special *Brené Brown: The Call to Courage,* "You cannot take criticism and feedback from people who are not being brave with their lives." She talks in her research about how being brave actually means being vulnerable. If people aren't in the ring with you, also being their truest and most vulnerable selves, they should not have any say in how you create your reality.

Haters are haters because they are not *makers:* They create nothing, rather, they hide behind their wall of negativity, trying to take you down instead of being vulnerable with others and with themselves.

It's okay, and even good, to surround yourself with people who offer constructive criticism and feedback. But only the people who know, love, and are invested in you deserve to give you that help. And if they're not? If they're just haters? Well, then you can shake them off.

## GOOD MORNING

When I was a teenager, on the weekends, my dad and I would often go on morning walks together. Sometimes we'd drive to the beach and walk back and forth along the sand for a few hours before stopping to eat huevos rancheros. Other times, we would grab the dogs and walk along the river near our house. No matter where we were walking, I found myself frequently embarrassed because my dad said good morning to everyone who passed.

The idea that my dad would bother random people, and interrupt our time together, by saying good morning to strangers was more than my teenage self could handle. And yet now, as an adult, I understand why he wanted this point of connection with others.

I have since gone on walks and forced myself to say good morning to everyone who passed me. My experience, of course, is a bit different from my father's, as I am a young woman walking alone, but overall, I feel safer, happier, and even a little bit more human by taking a moment to interact with another living person. The experience is entirely different than when I go on walks and don't acknowledge anyone around me.

"Good morning" is simple. It's more than a plain "hello," but not quite as personal as a "how are you doing?" It's acceptable to say in passing without being overbearing. More than anything, "good morning" is an invitation. It's an uncomplicated offering that says, "I see you." It is a gift. Despite its simplicity, it visibly impacts people. The most common response I received was delightful surprise: "Oh! Good morning to you, too."

Wherever your day starts out, try a few "good mornings" today. See what happens. Who doesn't want an invitation to be seen as a human being?

The country singer Reba McEntire said on the podcast Oprah's Master Class that you've got to have three bones in your life:

a wishbone . . . .

We must hope, not take ourselves too seriously, and never compromise on what we feel is right.

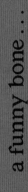

a funny bone . . .

Which of your bones needs
a little love right now?

and a back bone.

## MISE EN PLACE

Great chefs and even great home cooks practice mise en place, which, translated from the French, literally means "to put in place." Mise en place is a system of organization that demands that everything a chef needs to make a dish is prepared in advance—cleaned, chopped, measured out, and so on—and is immediately within her reach. It allows her the physical and mental space to be the most efficient by purposefully creating a space for her work.

Even if you are not a chef, you do some kind of work. And whether it is the type of work you are paid for or the work of your dreams that you do on the side, there are surely tools and routines necessary to your work. But how often do you think about the space you create to do that work as well as you can? How often is your work a result of convenience or habit versus intentional preparation?

Mise en place applies to the entirety of our lives, whether it's a space, a ritual, or a routine—mental or physical—to help you do your best work. We all enjoy the feeling of flow, the just-right groove of work.

Add mise en place to your routine and see what happens.

**GIVE PEOPLE TIME TO COME AROUND**

When I first came out to my mom, she cried. She was worried I would never have the kind of happiness she wanted for me: a lavish wedding, a kind husband, loving children. Now she posts pride flags on her Instagram feed with the caption **"Love is love."**

Sometimes people need some time to come around to new ideas. You might be catching them off guard, sharing a brand-new perspective with them. A visceral reaction isn't necessarily a final reaction. Even if you're comfortable with and used to the idea of whatever information you're sharing, remember that you weren't always in that position. Your audience might need—and deserves—time to process and reassess their previous views. It doesn't mean they won't ever come around. They just need a little bit of time.

## TEN YEARS, TEN THOUSAND HOURS

The average fruit tree doesn't produce any fruit for five to ten years. That's ten years of growing. Ten years during which the tree needs water, soil, and sun every day before it becomes productive. You wouldn't cut a tree down right before it produces fruit. And yet we treat ourselves with much less grace.

The author Malcolm Gladwell has written much about the principle of ten thousand hours. To become a true master of any skill, you must spend ten thousand hours honing your craft. He says that if you spend twenty hours a week on your skill, it will take you, yes, ten years to master it. Ten years of working to produce fruit.

We've all become used to instant gratification, so much so that when it's time to do the real work, we abandon the job because the progress doesn't feel fast enough—our impatience overshadows our drive. But it's not only that. It's also our belief that we are not actually successful until we've produced "fruit." But dedicating yourself to the work—during those ten years, or however long it takes you—is part of the progress.

Your work, like the tree's, is not frivolous. You're putting in your ten thousand hours, your ten years, in preparation for enjoying the fruits of your labor.

**GETTING GROUNDED**

Existential grounding is a technique that can alleviate a stressful day. My therapist described it to me through the lens of pets. Pets provide existential grounding because they show us there is a way to live other than our own. They calm us down and remind us that the pressures in our lives are largely of our own making.

Observe something today that is alive but not human: a dog, a cat, a bee, a flower, a tree, or whatever else you like. Let its existence wash over you. Let it ground you.

everything

in

moderation,

even

moderation

**DON'T BE A CHEAP COPY OF SOME-ONE ELSE**

My very first day of writing at BuzzFeed, I was uncertain of what I had to say just yet. I passed the hours looking at the top posts that were trending, and I tried my best to mimic them.

At the end of the day, when I turned my post in to my boss, he read my work and said, "This is great, but we already have it. Don't be a cheap copy of someone else when you can be the only version of yourself."

That lesson has stuck with me. It's one thing to seek inspiration from others, but another to just do what they've already done. Give the world your best version of you.

**FIKA** Sweden has a tradition known as "fika," which is a social meeting, usually over coffee accompanied by some kind of sweet. In America, we usually drink coffee alone at the beginning of the day, en route somewhere, or occasionally with company for a quick break. Fika is a more intentional meeting. Fika is more than a simple coffee break; it's a social recharge, a time meant for community. Even people who prefer to fika alone do so within a community.

Of course, this concept exists in other countries. The UK loves a pot of tea; India a nice masala chai; a post-meal mint tea is preferred in Morocco, and so on. But fika in Sweden is a way of life. It's a necessity to be with one another, to talk and catch up—and not just over text or Instagram DMs. And the Swedes do it every day, sometimes several times! It is vital that they *be* with each other, make memories, and share space. Fika ensures the Swedes an ongoing connection to one another, a safeguard against loneliness and isolation. It is a reminder that we all need—and have—one another.

When was the last time you invited a friend out just to have a chat over coffee and a warm cinnamon bun for no reason other than to be together? Maybe today is a good day for a fika.

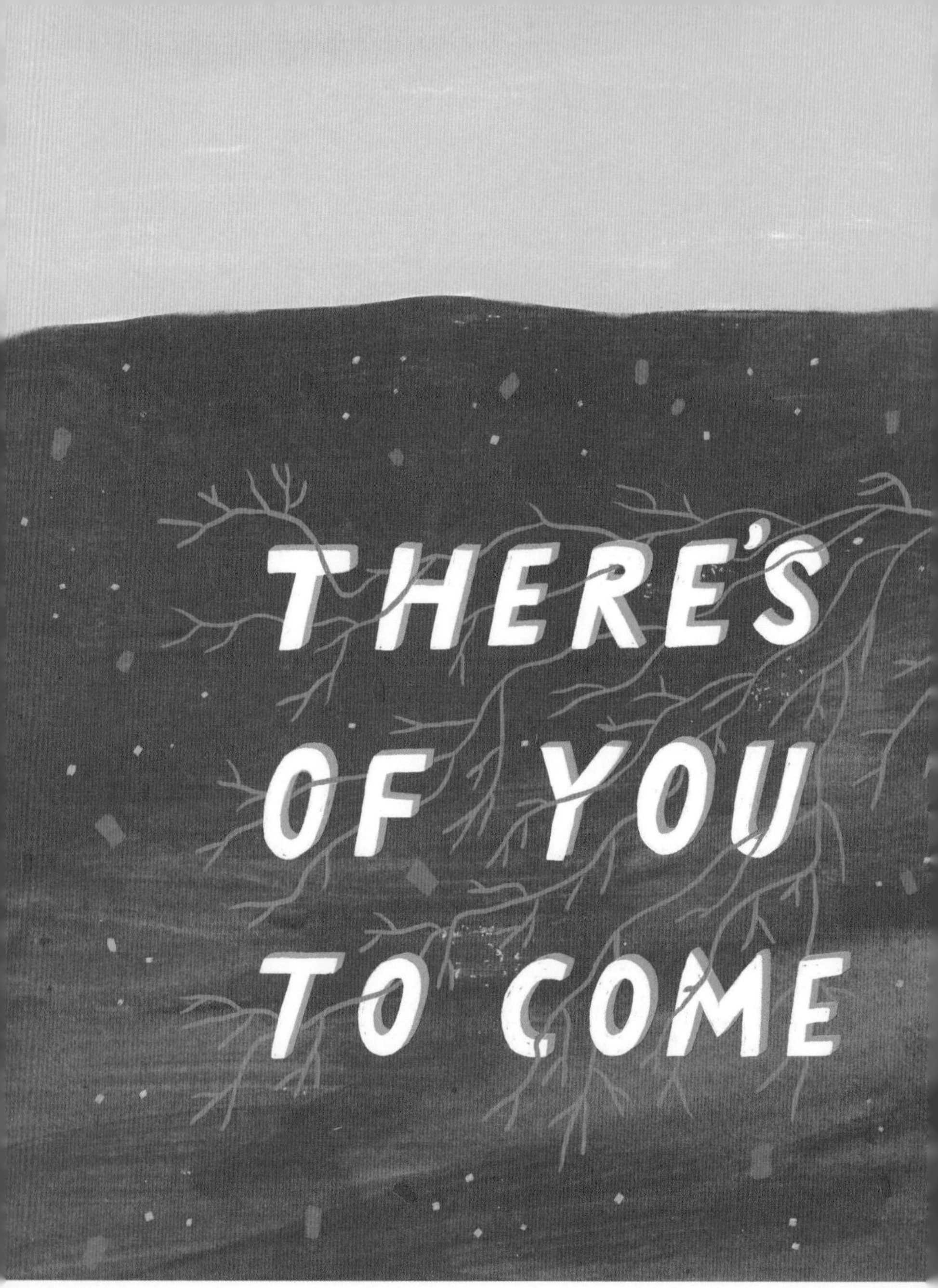
THERE'S
OF YOU
TO COME

STILL A LOT WAITING OUT.

## BASK IN YOUR SENSES

Staying present is difficult. We become so preoccupied with the past or the future that we forget the truly real moment is the one we're in at this very second.

When you are feeling overwhelmed, lost in your thoughts, dreams, and failures, or, for whatever other reason, not anchored to this moment in time, return to the simplest possible instruments of measurement you can: your senses.

Think about what you feel, smell, hear, see, and taste. Bask in those senses and take mental snapshots of your impressions. Get grounded. You are here now, and being here now is a gift.

## EVERY-THING MORE LIKE ITSELF

A common misconception is that salt adds its own flavor to food: add salt, and food becomes saltier—end of story. That is, in fact, not the end of salt's story.

Yes, it adds saltiness, but it also brings out the flavors of whatever food it's being added to. It releases hidden aromas, reduces our perception of bitterness, and reveals to us tastes that, before salting, weren't present. Essentially, salt makes things taste more like themselves.

The danger of salt, however, is that there's a hidden threshold at which it ceases to bring out flavor and instead becomes the *only* flavor. Once a dish is oversalted, it's nearly impossible to bring the intended flavors back. You can't taste anything else.

People are a lot like salt: At their best, they add immense flavor to your life, bringing out a side you hadn't necessarily known before and making you feel more like yourself. But at their worst, they bring so much of themselves that they try to change you, oversalting you until none of your own flavor remains.

Don't let yourself be oversalted. Keep people around you who add just the right amount of seasoning, people who reveal and release what's within you. And, just as important, do the same for others.

## WHERE'S THE CIRCUS?

Frida Kahlo, the iconic, bisexual, disabled Mexican artist, created some of the twentieth century's most recognizable art. She was best known for self-portraits, which often included extremely graphic depictions of the female reality, including her own miscarriage.

During her lifetime, Frida, uncompromising both personally and politically, was not always understood, nor was she always respected. Known for her colorful wardrobe, mainly comprised of traditional Tehuana dresses, she certainly stood out. Children on the street would call out after her, *"Donde está el circo?"* or "Where is the circus?" Each time, she would simply respond with a smile.

This anecdote represents how little attention Frida paid to the conventions of her day; she didn't care what was popular or politically correct, an attitude that permeates her daring art. Despite being misunderstood as both a woman and a Mexican artist during her lifetime, her legacy endures to this day. Frida became the first twentieth-century Mexican artist whose work was acquired by the Louvre. In 2016, sixty-two years after her death, her painting *Two Nudes in a Forest* was sold by Christie's auction house for $8 million.

Today, bask in Frida's energy. Wear what you want, create what you want, and do what you want to do because <u>you</u> want to. Let your unapologetic sense of self be what leads you to your greatness.

# SECOND
# DRAFTS

I'm not a second-draft kind of girl. In most of my school-work, I put all of my effort and time into my first draft, then never went back to refine it. I was content with whatever grade I received, even when it wasn't the best, because putting in the extra effort necessary to close the gap to excellence didn't seem worth it. "An 89 percent is close enough to an A," I would tell myself, avoiding doing more work. But what I was really avoiding was the painful fear that maybe I wasn't good enough, maybe I wasn't perfect.

Let me explain. If I got a B+, but I didn't actually try that hard, having only done one draft, then I could still say I was doing fine. But if I had tried harder, tried my best to refine my work, only to find I still got a B+, then what could I say to myself? I would be a failure.

Doing the work is difficult. Going back to the second draft is tough, because it means admitting that we are not perfect, that we could have done better. It took me almost thirty years of living to accept this insanely obvi-ous truth: No one is perfect. Absolutely no one, including me, and including you.

We never get it exactly right on the first try. We all need second drafts, and sometimes third and fourth and fifth drafts, because we all benefit from giving ourselves the space to improve.

TAKE
THE
NOTES.

REVISE
THE
DRAFT.

AND IF YOU STILL GET A B+, KEEP GOING.

# FOUR THINGS

## MY CAT HAS TAUGHT ME ABOUT BEING HUMAN

**ALWAYS BE CURIOUS.** Something interesting is always happening around you. You just have to stop long enough to enjoy it.

**DO THINGS YOUR OWN WAY.** My cat doesn't care a single bit about what you want him to do. He operates completely on his own time and according to his own whims.

**DOING THINGS YOUR OWN WAY DOESN'T MAKE YOU A JERK.** A follow-up point to the above: Knowing what you want doesn't make you a bad person (or a bad cat). If you're a people pleaser, this lesson is critical to learn. Doing something for yourself, the way you want it, doesn't make you selfish—it just means you know what you want.

EVEN INDEPENDENT CREATURES NEED SNUGGLES. It's true that my cat is more independent than most, but he starts every day with twenty to thirty minutes of straight-up pets. Not just casual pets—luxurious pets. He basks in affection, and then when he's ready and recharged, he's on his merry way. Even if you're as independent as they come, be sure you still make time for connection.

Being stuck, by definition, means you can't move. But there's an important distinction between being stuck and being paralyzed.

I imagine being stuck as being trapped in a big, deep pile of wet mud—the kind it's tough to lift your feet from because of the tenacious, suction-like grip it has on your feet. You have to work crazy hard to pick a foot up, and it feels a bit like you're being pulled back down when you do. But being paralyzed is being truly incapacitated. "Paralyzed" is every muscle in your body tightening itself and never relieving that tension. "Paralyzed" is being instantly frozen, like what liquid nitrogen does to water.

*BOTH ARE SCARY.* What if I never move again? How can I live my life if I am here forever?

# MOVE WHEN YOU'RE STUCK

While it is certainly difficult to move forward when you're stuck, you have one saving grace: You can still move the rest of your body. In fact, your arms, torso, head, and your other leg muscles are essentially the only tools you have to gain the momentum and force needed to unstick yourself. You must move! It's the only way out. And any motion is better than none.

If you're staring at a blank page, incapable of thinking of a single thing to write, jot down anything, even if it's gibberish, just so you can get out of the headspace of staring at the blank page that represents your current failure. If you're cleaning your bathroom and you feel overwhelmed by the sheer amount of toiletries you've accumulated, pick one that you know you don't need and throw it away.

But whatever you do, don't stay in the panic, don't stay in the stuck. Often, the anxiety of being stuck is worse than the stuckness itself.

> The next time you feel paralyzed, consider whether there's some way you can move. Even if it's not forward, at least it's something to get yourself unstuck.

**NOURISH YOUR SOUL**

When I was twenty-two, I taught English in South Korea for a year. Despite my heritage, I'm sad to say that I didn't know any Korean going into the year. Therefore, I was beguiled by one particular phrase that came up almost every day I was there. "밥 먹었어요?" *Bap mogossoyo?* Literally translated, it means "Have you eaten rice?"

It seems like a straightforward question, I know—only that's not actually what it means. Used colloquially, this phrase means "How are you?" Teachers would ask me this when I walked into class, friends would ask this when I sat down for a meal, and sometimes even clerks at the grocery store would ask. "Have you eaten rice?"

The origin of this idiom is somewhat literal. After the Korean War, when Korea was the poorest country in the world, people would ask each other, "Have you eaten rice?" and mean it. The question was meant to ensure you were well. Have you eaten? Are you okay? Can I help? Over time, like all things, the phrase changed. Now, the literal phrase asks an emotional question.

You know how hard it can be to answer a simple "How are you?" "Good. Fine." Even when, in fact, you're not good at all. In some ways, the Korean version of this common greeting solidified to me what was missing from its English counterpart. To be "good," to be "fine," you have to be well fed, sustained, to have eaten rice—or whatever it is in your own life that gives you nourishment. That could be buying flowers, sitting with your pet, or calling a friend for a catch-up.

H*W IS
YOUR S*UL?
IS IT FULL?
HAVE YOU
EATEN RICE
T*DAY?

# JUST

## WHEN I WANT SOMETHING, I ASK FOR IT.

I don't sit around and contemplate whether I should be asking or whether I'm deserving of such an opportunity. Particularly as women, we often talk ourselves out of action in our contemplation. *I'll do this later. Maybe next week. After I have more experience. When the timing is better.* But while we sit around and contemplate action, other people are out there doing—they are asking. And, in return, they're getting what they want.

Why is that? Often, the fear of asking is simply the fear of rejection—what if the powers that be say no? What if they laugh? I'll tell you right now what will

# A S K

happen . . . are you ready? Really ready? Okay, here it is: **They'll say no, and then you'll move on.** That's it. No harm, no foul, just a single no (for now, at least—a no isn't always forever).

If we shed the fear of hearing no, there is virtually nothing we will be afraid to ask, whether in dating, careers, friendship, or anything else. All asking does is get you an answer. It removes you from the "what if" and into the "what now" or "what next." Instead of feeling fear of hearing no, feel grateful for the clarity that no—or yes—provides.

**JUST ASK.**

## EVERYONE'S
### A CELEBRITY

My mom, Cookie, lives her life in a different way than the average person. One day when I was in high school, she was driving me to school in our Nissan Quest minivan, and I noticed there was a birthday cake strapped into the seat next to me. "Happy birthday Graciela," it read.

"Who's Graciela?" I asked my mom, confused.

"Oh, she's my friend at the Enterprise car rental. Today's her birthday. She's turning twenty-seven."

Enterprise car rental. How often are you renting a car near your home? We had done so once, about three years prior. Not only had my mom remembered Graciela's birthday, but she was also bringing her a cake to celebrate. I kid you not.

To my mom, celebrities don't exist. Rather, everyone is interesting, and everyone is deserving of her time. This approach has brought my mom a lot of free things in life—a lot of good karma thrown back her way—but that's not why she does it. She is kind to you because you are a person and therefore you deserve kindness.

Is there someone not usually on your radar whom you might be able to make feel like a celebrity today?

The first time I was labeled a dilettante, it was not meant in a nice way. *Dilettante* is defined by Merriam-Webster as "a person having a superficial interest in an art or a branch of knowledge." My boss called me this in a conversation about whether or not to promote me; he was worried that my ever-changing interests would prevent me from committing to any one project and therefore from achieving any real success.

To some degree, he was right. I was definitely a dabbler—and yet his quick categorization of me still felt wrong. I explored a multitude of subjects because of my curiosity, not because of impatience. So, when I looked up this word that had been hurled at me to try to keep me down, I was surprised.

A dilettante, by definition, is a jack of all trades and master of none, but the word is derived from the present participle of *dilettare*, Italian for "to delight in." Now, that I could relate to. I was certainly a delighter at heart! And what's wrong with delight? Isn't the point of being alive to delight in as much as we possibly can?

Perhaps you are like me, overwhelmed by all there is to delight in in this world. Too many countries to visit, too many books to read, too much music, TV, art, and friendships. But perhaps that's okay—perhaps we are meant to delight, to follow our curiosities, to explore. Let's delight together in all our universe has to offer.

## ACCELERATE WHEN YOU'RE TIRED

James Dyson was largely rejected when he developed the world's first bagless vacuum cleaner. In the early 1980s, when he presented the concept for his invention to Hoover and Electrolux, the giant brands leading the industry at the time, he was dismissed outright. No one thought he was especially smart for reinventing technology that didn't seem to need reinventing.

But Dyson believed his product was superior and could reimagine the vacuum market. On his way to the final product, he made 5,127 prototypes. Now, Dyson makes a lot more than vacuums, and his net worth is over $5 billion. *He* is the giant brand leading the game.

When asked about his success on the NPR podcast *How I Built This,* Dyson compared it to the time he spent doing long-distance running in school. He said that, aside from a great amount of training, long-distance running is mostly about stamina. When you feel tired is exactly when you should accelerate—the other runners are also tired; if you accelerate at your lowest point, that's when you'll start winning.

Your talent alone won't get you through any race; it's your stamina that will separate you from your competitors.

Don't give up.
Keep it up.
Accelerate.

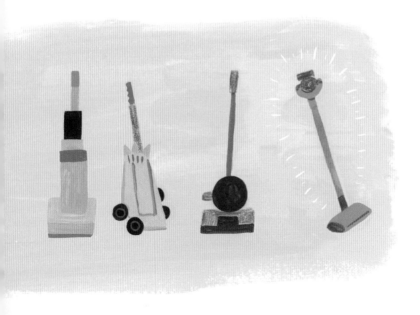

hope

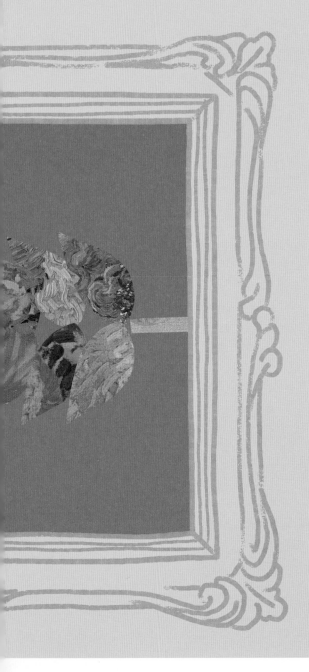

In 1885, the painter Vincent van Gogh remarked to his brother Theo in a letter regarding his art, "If I am worth anything later, I am worth something now. For wheat is wheat, even if it looks like grass at first."

Even if it's not clear to everyone else what you're doing or how you're going to be successful, know that you own your value—it is not assigned by anyone else. You know you are wheat even if all that's visible right now is a blade of grass.

## THE BEAUTY IN GRIEVING

The Portuguese word *saudade* means "a melancholic longing," especially for a time that either never really happened or a time that will never return. *Saudade* has been more succinctly described as the presence of absence.

We have all lost someone or something: a dream, a grandparent, a pet, a friend, a job, our health, a parent, a child. We've all had that terrible pain, the ache that doesn't seem to go away. And most days, it feels impossible not to ask, Is there any good in this pain? What is the point of all this missing?

In some ways, the only part of grief that is beautiful is its presence, because it means we once had something so rich and beautiful that its absence from our life has left us with a kind of *saudade* that never quite goes away. We cannot get back the ones we loved, the dreams we lost, or the moments gone by. But we can bask in the presence that is their absence and be grateful that we have something to miss in the first place.

## DON'T WASTE YOUR TIME ON TOXIC PEOPLE

Oprah said the best advice she ever got was from Maya Angelou, who told her, "When people show you who they are, believe them." If someone is consistently rude, unkind, harsh, or demanding, they will likely never change, and certainly not on your behalf. When you're a trusting person, it's difficult to believe that the people who hurt you are wrong in doing so. It's easy to excuse their behavior, to give them a pass due to a "bad day," or even to think they're acting appropriately. But listen to Maya Angelou. Believe people when they show you who they are.

Instead of giving your time to people who don't treat you the right way, take it back. Keep it for yourself—or give it to those who build and lift you up.

In the Bible, Ecclesiastes 3:11 states, "He has made everything beautiful in its time." A 1997 Indigo Girls song more simply states, "Everything in its own time" (and that's the name of the song, too).

What I take away from these similar sentiments is that, by definition, your time cannot be dictated by anyone else's timing. Your life, your path, your journey, and your joy are singularly your own. Everything that is yours will be made beautiful in *your* own time.

Don't dwell on someone else's life, and don't let someone else control yours. Instead, rest assured that your completion will come when you are ready for it. In its own time.

# IN ITS OWN TIME

# ENJOY THE PROCESS

If you've never seen a sand mandala, I suggest you put this book down and look up a picture of one right now. A mandala (Sanskrit for "circle") is a work of art that Buddhist monks use to contemplate the impermanence of life. They'll spend hours upon hours, for days and even weeks, crafting an elaborate and impossible work of sand art—only to, upon completion, blow the entire thing away. All that work, all that meticulous effort, is gone in seconds.

So why do it in the first place?

Sometimes the work is the journey, and the process is the part we're supposed to learn from. Like the mandala, the results of our work may one day be gone, too, but that shouldn't discourage us from undertaking it.

Nature is not selfish. It doesn't hoard, conserve, or wait to see if it needs something before it passes along its resources. In fact, it cannot be selfish: The laws of thermodynamics demand that nature shares, that there is balance.

For example, heat must be passed to whatever surrounding molecules have less heat. That's why ice cubes melt, fire keeps you warm, and hot sun streaming into a car makes the leather seats too toasty to sit on. Heat is generous in this way, always giving.

Trees are the same. The tallest trees in the forest, which receive the most sunlight and thus photosynthesize the most sugar, share that sugar with the fungi network growing on top of their roots. Those fungi, deep underground, need sugar to stay alive, and yet they cannot produce their own beneath the soil. The tree not only provides it, but then it also shares its sugars with the smaller surrounding trees through that underground fungi network—so the fungi are generous, too.

This sharing doesn't make heat less hot; it doesn't make a tree less of a tree.

**BE GENEROUS TODAY.**

**GIVE SOMETHING AWAY.**

**WHAT LASTS** When Gustave Eiffel, Maurice Koechlin, and Émile Nouguier first built the Eiffel Tower, it was only meant to be a temporary structure for the 1889 World's Fair in Paris. It has now been standing for over 130 years.

You never know what is going to resonate with others. When it comes to your own ideas, be unbiased. Don't underestimate your passing thoughts, your just-for-practices, your not-meant-to-lasts. They might be the most lasting of all.

# WATER

Water comes in three different forms: solid, liquid, and gas. Water can clink in your glass, hang heavy in the rainforest, or make waves for surfers to ride—radically different existences. You, too, don't have to be the same person all the time. You, too, can change.

# DONE

☒ IS

☐ IS NOT

# BETTER THAN PERFECT

There is a false and infectious idea in creative work that joy comes only from making something good. While it undoubtedly feels good to create something you like, don't discount the simple joy of finishing something.

I am a perfectionist. Rather than help me create perfect art, perfectionism has left me with a graveyard of half-finished projects, all stopped at the point when they got too hard or began to stray from the vision in my mind.

During my last semester of college, I had to write a fifty-page senior thesis. I had months to work on it but, of course, two weeks before graduation, I somehow had only twelve pages written. I had spent so much time trying to make those twelve pages perfect that I hadn't gotten past them. Then, while procrastinating on Pinterest, I came across a quote: "Done is better than perfect." These words refocused my priorities. My motivation shifted from perfection to just being finished. I worked at a breakneck pace those last two weeks of college, and eventually I completed my thesis. No matter the quality of the work, it was done.

**WHAT CAN YOU FINISH TODAY?**

Yes, there is merit in doing good work and making art, but there is also merit in simply finishing. Because whether the project is "good" or "bad," you did it.

## THERE'S ALWAYS MORE TO LEARN

My abuelo died in June 2019. Rafael Perez Martinez was the wisest person I've ever met. He spent his life dedicated to two things: family and the pursuit of knowledge. His house was filled with thousands of books—all of which he had read, and all of which he could recite by memory. Everyone who knew him referred to him as "the walking encyclopedia."

I was his first grandchild, and throughout my life, we would write letters to each other to catch up and practice my Spanish. Here is some of the best advice he gave me, quoted directly from a letter he wrote me in 2015:

*"Nunca creas saberlo todo—siempre necesitamos aprender más."*

Never think you know everything—we must always learn more.

If that isn't the most beautiful part about being alive, I'm not sure what is.

NUNCA CREAS
SABERLO TODO–
SIEMPRE
NECESITAMOS
APRENDER
MÁS.

PRODUCTION:

ROLL:

SCENE:

TAKE:

4,561 EPISODES

DATE:

The creative process can be unrelenting. Whenever it bums me out, I think about the fact that Oprah recorded 4,561 episodes of *The Oprah Winfrey Show* over the course of twenty-five years, and yet only a handful of moments are considered iconic. Meaning that most of the work Oprah did on her show was unremarkable—yet that doesn't mean it was unimportant.

When talking about her work in a 2017 issue of *Vogue*, Oprah said, "Do the work as an offering, and then whatever happens, happens." Oprah didn't know which of her 4,561 episodes of *The Oprah Winfrey Show* would be culture-changing or life-altering for her audience, but she recorded them all anyway.

Creatives often fall into the trap of assigning immense value to their own work, treating each piece as if it will be *the one* that changes the world. We pour in our hopes, ideals, and dreams, and we are disappointed when no one cares. We ask why we work at all and if we should keep going.

The answer is: of course. If you love something, do it for the love of the work. Do your work as an offering, not for praise, pomp, or recognition—that's your part. The rest is up to the universe.

don't
wait
for
someone
else
to
fix it

I once had the privilege of participating in a small discussion with Gloria Steinem, one of the essential leaders of the feminist movement, about the intersections among women, activism, and art. I asked her, "What is an activist? What do we have to do to call ourselves 'activists'?" She replied simply, "Find something that's annoyingly unfair, and don't wait for someone else to fix it."

You may not yet feel like a changemaker, a leader, or an activist today, but surely there is some injustice in the world that annoys the crap out of you. What are you going to do about it?

**DISFRUTA**   Nothing is more appetizing to me than a ripe mango. When I was a kid, my dad would cut them up in his own special way, which made them even more enjoyable to eat. First, he would cut around the pit, splitting the mango into halves. Then he would score each half with a grid of little squares until, finally, he flipped it inside out and handed it to me to eat. Today, as an adult, I still get giddy while eating mangoes.

In Spanish, the word for enjoy is *disfrutar,* a word that has the same root as the word for *fruit.* In Latin, *fructus* means "something you enjoy." When I was young, I found it funny when people said *disfruta* because to me it seemed like they were saying enjoy your fruit or, specifically in my case, enjoy your mangoes. Now that I know my way around these words, I love that visualization because it's literal. We should be enjoying everything and every moment the way we enjoy our favorite fruits—savoring every bite, treasuring the experience of simply eating our proverbial mangoes.

## <u>Disfruta!</u>
## Go enjoy something
## like it's fruit today.

EVEN A PAWN

In the game of chess,
every piece has its
own special super-
power. If you feel like
a pawn today, know
that you are meant
to be exactly who you
are, with exactly the
gifts you have, and
there's no reason
you can't be the one
to win the game.
Even a pawn can take
down a king!

**YOU NEED REST**

I'm not good at resting. In fact, I have attention-deficit/hyperactivity disorder (ADHD)—emphasis on the hyperactivity.

Stillness does not exist in my bones, literally, and because of this, I am also not very patient. I rush everything—truly everything—that can be rushed. I brush my teeth in thirty seconds, drink my coffee without concern for burning my tongue, and tie my shoes so fast that they often come untied later. I even have difficulty reading the ends of sentences, because I'm too impatient to finish them.

Given all of that, I never thought of rest as anything but a waste of time. Why would you rest when you could keep going? Get on with it!

But rest is not wasteful. It's not lost time between bursts of productivity. **Rest *is* a step.**

Consider bread as an example. A crucial step in baking bread is proofing, during which the yeast begins to ferment, causing the dough to rise. Most breads, after being mixed and kneaded, need to proof for at least an hour. What does that entail? Quite literally, nothing. It's time to set the bread aside and leave it to rest. Time to let it do its thing.

We forget that rest is part of the process. It's not lost time; it's an absolutely necessary part of whatever you're doing. We cannot always be primed and productive; we need mental marination. It's vital.

## A GOOD BUBBLE

"Staying inside your bubble" has negative connotations. To most people, it means that you're isolating yourself from new ideas, staying within your comfort zone, and fending off anything foreign. You're closed off, more concerned with being safe than with learning.

I'd like to offer up a different type of bubble—a good bubble. Did you know it's possible to have a sustained fire underwater? Yes, a screaming hot, jumping flame, underwater fire. All you need is a bubble.

Underwater welders work in the ocean repairing ships, oil rigs, and fiber-optic cables. They are able to do their jobs because two pressurized gases meet at the tip of the welding gun and form not only a flame, but also a bubble around it, giving the flame air to live and breathe.

Clearly, some bubbles are good. You might not be literally trying to tend a fire underwater, but maybe you are trying to light up while you're feeling submerged. You might need protection from the forces that are trying to keep you down, to extinguish your inner fire. Think of your bubble not as keeping the bad forces out but, instead, as keeping what you need near you. Use your protective bubble to surround yourself with the positivity you need to keep your spark lit.

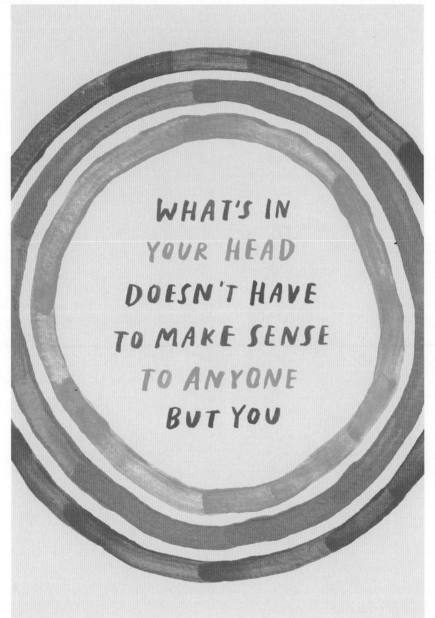

WHAT'S IN
YOUR HEAD
DOESN'T HAVE
TO MAKE SENSE
TO ANYONE
BUT YOU

# FIRST
# THINGS
# FIRST

When I was twenty-six, I decided I wanted to learn how to boulder (it's essentially the same thing as indoor rock climbing but without the safety ropes). As with any new task, there were approximately 17,932 details to remember: how to grip a hold, how to breathe evenly so as not to freeze halfway up the wall, where to put my feet, how to chalk my hands, how to fall safely so I don't die, and so on and so forth.

Every time I would try to solve a problem (that's what you call it when you're trying to climb up a path—another thing to remember), I found myself completely overwhelmed and frustrated. The tasks were not automatic for me at all, so every small climb felt like Mount Everest. Then, one day, my friend Henry told me it didn't need to be so hard. "Just focus on one thing at a time. Eventually that will become automatic, and you can work on the next thing." He was right: Of course, you can't learn everything about something new all at once.

Learning requires a steep curve. We want to master skills quickly and easily so we can become experts as fast as we can dream. But the truth is that everything is extremely difficult the first time you do it—and, if we're being honest, the first hundred times you do it. But if you give yourself room to conquer one detail, eventually you'll find that without even thinking about it, you can do the thing that was impossible.

When Steve Jobs decided to drop out of Reed College, he was making one of the most important decisions he would ever make, but not for the reason you might think. Because Jobs had dropped out of college and therefore regular coursework, he was free to audit whatever classes he found interesting rather than those necessary for filling requirements. One class that caught his eye was calligraphy. Intricate, hand-lettered posters advertising school events hung everywhere around campus, and he was curious about the craft behind the art. He enrolled and soon learned about the spacing between the letters, the differences between serif and sans-serif scripts, and the delicacy of different letter combinations. He was taken by every bit of it.

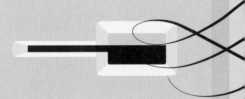

BEAUTIFUL
ACCIDENTS

Years later, when Jobs was designing the first Apple computer, he purposefully included beautiful typography in addition to the practical fonts that were being used in computers at the time. Had he not dropped out of college and audited that calligraphy class, it's possible none of our computers would include artistic fonts alongside the pragmatic ones.

It's impossible to know which of our seemingly small choices will have the biggest impact moving forward. We can't know what random collection of experiences, people, and conversations will create magic for us. Most of the time, we don't know those moments are happening in real time—that we're meeting people who will change our lives, having conversations that will change our perspectives, or making choices that might change the world.

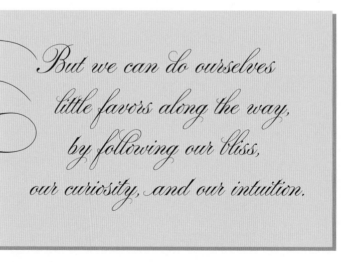

*But we can do ourselves little favors along the way, by following our bliss, our curiosity, and our intuition.*

ENJOY TODAY

EVERYTHING

★

CHANGES

ONE DAY

YOU WILL MISS

RIGHT NOW

# WHAT IS YOU

One of the first classes I took in college was a seminar on vocation. I'd never heard the word *vocation* before, so I looked it up to learn that it's just a fancy name for an occupation. At that point, I was sure my "vocation" would be advertising, because after watching Helen Hunt come up with that Nike campaign where the woman is running on pavement in the early-morning mist in the 2000 movie *What Women Want*, advertising was all I wanted to do. But during this course, I realized that a vocation is more than a job. A vocation is your calling, derived from the Latin *vocare*, which means "to call." It is the job we feel we are meant to do.

The idea of a calling daunts me. Even in my thirties, I feel ill prepared to take on something as big as that. Isn't a calling reserved for special people? People like Barack Obama, Oprah, or Beyoncé? What could I possibly be called for?

# R CALLING?

We all have a calling to ourselves. Toni Morrison says in an interview on Oprah.com that our job as free people is to free other people. That if we have power, our job is to empower someone else. Because beyond our job titles, our real job is to improve the well-being of those around us in the time we get to live this life. No matter our job, our vocation is to understand as much about ourselves as we can and then to share that real empathy with the world. Empathy changes reality—it opens up human connection in a way no other emotion can.

When you look at it this way, you know you don't have to be Beyoncé to have a calling. You realize that your calling is coming from inside the house. It's not some grand light that will shine down on you and show you the way. Your vocation is an invitation into your own spirit. So bring your best humanity; that is your calling.

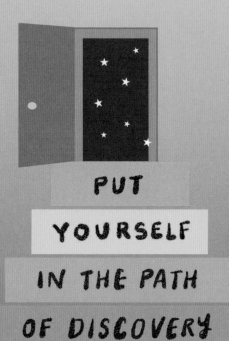

PUT YOURSELF IN THE PATH OF DISCOVERY

Sometimes novelty is just about being creative and finding new ways to put yourself in the path of discovery. In case you're hard-pressed for ideas, here are a few you could do today.

Download the TED app and listen to a randomly chosen talk. Guaranteed you'll learn something new.

Call your mom, your dad, or an old friend on the way to or from work and ask them to tell you a story about them you don't already know.

Purposefully take a new route home, to work, or to school and just observe how that route is different from your usual one.

## Happy discovering!

With some things, it may seem there is only one way to do it. Everyone may appear to do some things one specific way.

# THERE ARE A MILLION WAYS TO DO EVERY-THING.

DO THINGS

*There isn't. They don't.*

Do things that ignite your sense of joy; do things because they make you happy or curious.

DO THINGS HOW YOU WANT TO DO THEM.

UNCONVENTIONALLY

A TOM
KIND

# HANKS
# OF DAY

*Continued on next page*

When I decided to move to New York City in 2013, I thought I would have Tom Hanks and Meg Ryan kinds of days all the time. I imagined my life would feel like I was inside a Nora Ephron movie, complete with its own whimsical soundtrack and quirky voice-overs. Instead of all that, I felt more depressed than ever before. I had lived in California for the majority of my life, and I found not having a support system nearby very difficult. I was lonely in a city of 10 million strangers.

So, on a day when I was tired of feeling depressed, I hopped on the subway and took it straight to Times Square. Now, actual New Yorkers almost never go to Times Square—not unless they absolutely have to—but I didn't have anywhere else to go that day. I figured I would buy a cheap ticket to a Broadway show and see a musical alone.

By the time I arrived at the Times Square train station, I was hot, sweaty, and hungry, and I was debating whether I should simply turn around and go home. I decided not to—I'd already come all this way. When I finally exited the station, I was greeted by a giant billboard of Tom Hanks. There he was—I had found him! And, believe it or not, this was his Broadway debut, in the very last play Ephron wrote before she died, *Lucky Guy*. The moment felt like a little gift from the universe, a sign to keep going. And then!

As I walked down West 44th Street to investigate my sign from the universe, Tom Hanks stepped out of the stage door, and suddenly he was standing right in front of me—in the flesh. "Oh, hello," he said, looking me straight in the eye. I appeared to be the only person in the middle of what should have been a bustling New York City street to witness this. "Thanks for coming out. Are you here to see the show?" he asked, very Tom Hanksily.

In every sense of the word, I was flabbergasted. "I want to, but I don't have a ticket. The sign says it's sold out."

"Oh, that's all right. They usually hold back some standing-room tickets, and they're cheaper. Follow me."

Tom Hanks walked me to the box office and told the woman behind the counter that this young lady (me!) would like a standing-room ticket to today's show. Then he said he hoped I enjoyed the show, and he politely excused himself. And that was how I had the Tom Hanks / Nora Ephron (Meg Ryan in spirit) day of my dreams on what had started out as my lowest day in New York.

This story is fun to share, but it's also a reminder that sometimes the universe has a way of giving you exactly what you need—and that sometimes you have to put yourself out there to help it, even when you don't feel like doing a thing.

How can you help the universe help you?

**BANANA BREAD** You know that moment when a perfectly ripe banana is suddenly covered in dark brown spots? You waited too long to eat it. And now it'll go to waste. Or maybe not.

When you're making banana bread, only the spottiest, most bruised, mushiest banana will do. It's exactly the things that make it unappealing to eat that make it perfect for baking. And so, the banana's second act begins.

There's always a way to reinvent yourself. Embrace your dark spots for the sweetness they bring, and jump into Act II.

hope

work

I spent my first few years after college in a total panic, unable to find a job that made sense as a stepping-stone to the life I wanted as an artist. I worked as a bus driver, as the office manager at my dad's dental practice, and as an English teacher in South Korea. Eventually, I found my way to becoming an editorial fellow at BuzzFeed in 2013, but even now, after I've come and gone from that chapter in my life, I still find myself encountering professional crossroads, worried again that I'll make a wrong choice.

To reassure myself, I think of what Julianne Moore said when asked by Kim Masters on the podcast *The Business* about why she took a job as a soap opera actor for three years when she wanted to be known as a serious actor. She responded, "Work. Just work. You don't have to be somewhere forever, but you learn a lot by just actually working."

Julianne Moore has one of the most enviable careers in Hollywood—and she's gotten there by never having stopped working. No job is forever, and there's plenty to take away from each one. Whenever you find yourself at a crossroads, wondering if you're going to make a decision that will somehow screw up your whole life, just do the work.

## LITTLE
## JOYS

I loved shopping for school supplies when I was in grade school. A specific and certain rush came along with carefully selecting pens, binders, folders, notebooks, and the perfect backpack. It gave me the feeling that anything was possible at the start of a new school year.

Yes, I miss that feeling of possibility, but, to be honest, I also really miss the pens. More than any other school supply, I've always been attached to pens. At my school, we weren't allowed to write with a pen until fifth grade, and, even then, we were required to buy only erasable pens. We couldn't use the real, permanent kind until seventh grade.

I love pens with fine tips, gentle rolling ink that sits wet on the page for a moment. I love felt-tip pens, in a rainbow of colors, that squish into the paper as you press them down. I love gel pens and hotel pens and simple blue ballpoint pens that work really well on the first try.

As an adult—when pens were no longer a novelty to me—I largely accepted whatever pens were nearby, using the generic sort provided in my office, whatever was lying around at the DMV or the bank, whatever pen had found its way into my house. Then, one day, I saw my agent Carolyn using a red marking pen on a clean, white, cardboard pad, and I was immediately overcome with jealousy. I loved that pen. I wanted that pen! And then it dawned on me that I could, indeed, go get myself that pen, and I could experience pleasure every time I wrote with it. So I took myself pen shopping, and it was absolutely glorious.

I don't use pens that I don't like anymore, at least when I can help it. I always keep a pen I love at the ready.

We forget to take joy from the seemingly mundane or small things we love. It's okay to have a favorite pen, gardening tool, spatula, T-shirt, pair of socks—you name it. We are allowed to indulge, especially when it's easy.

## What's your "pen"?
## What easy joy can you
## add to your life?

**REALLY**
**SIMPLE**
**ADVICE**
**FOR A**
**REALLY**
**ROUGH**
**DAY**

Some advice is so simple—so easy and so unequivocally true—that you respond, "Oh, yes, of course," and you wonder why you didn't think of it yourself.

That's how I feel about Tracee Ellis Ross's advice for hard times. She says in an Instagram post:

When I'm having a really rough day, or a really bad moment, I have three tips:

1. *Change your underwear.*
2. *Wash your face.*
3. *Look at a tree.*

That's it. Of course, you can do those three things— even on the worst of days. If you're having a rough time of it, don't take my advice. Take Tracee's.

## MORNING PAGES

One of my favorite artistic catalysts is a practice called "morning pages." Created by Julia Cameron, author of *The Artist's Way*, morning pages is a tool to clear out all of the thoughts clouding your head so you can begin to make art. Cameron asks that every morning you journal three pages of unfiltered writing. It truly doesn't matter what the words say as long as the entry is three pages long.

Especially if you practice this every day, you'll be surprised by what and how much comes out. I found that, at first, it was all my insecurities—my deepest, darkest fears come to life. Then, eventually, after writing three pages every day, I got sick of writing about my insecurities and started coming up with actual ideas.

That's the point: You get all the junk out of your head so you can get to the real art of it all.

Getting started is a bit like running a hose that hasn't been turned on for a while. At first, there's a lot of sputtering, a lot of dirt, leaves, and debris—until, finally, the sputtering stops, and clear water flows.

RUNNING
PURELY
ON
PASSION

Jane Goodall was not an expert when she began researching chimpanzees in 1957. She wasn't a researcher, she had never been to university, and she had no special qualifications—other than a life-long passion for animals and a willingness to learn.

Goodall began studying chimpanzees at a time when they had never been seriously studied before—not by any man and certainly not by an unqualified twenty-six-year-old woman. In the jungle, she studied them from afar for months and months until she gained the chimps' trust and was granted access to the heart of their home, a place no human had entered before.

Goodall's still-ongoing study is the longest running of any animal in their natural habitat ever. She has made history many times over. What I love most about Goodall is that she managed to achieve the extraordinary by running purely on passion. She was a simple girl who grew up loving animals, and she followed that joy until it led to invaluable achievements. Where will your passion take you?

## YOU DON'T HAVE TO BE GOOD AT EVERYTHING

I once had a friend who, for her whole life, wanted to be "good at plants." No matter how many beautiful houseplants she bought, no matter how many articles she read about taking care of them, they all died. Eventually, she stopped buying plants, until one day, someone recommended that she try growing succulents. So she did. And to her surprise, they didn't die. (You might be thinking that it's impossible to kill a succulent, but I can tell you from personal experience that it's definitely not.)

You don't have to be good at all things in general—you can just be good at one thing. You don't have to be "just not a plant person"; you can be "a succulent person." If you feel like you haven't quite found your niche yet, it doesn't mean you're way off base in your searching. Get more specific and keep diving into what you love.

# START
# TURNING
# OFF
# LIGHTS

A January 2018 episode of *The Director's Cut* features Spike Jonze interviewing Greta Gerwig about the release of her feature directorial debut, *Lady Bird*. Gerwig shares that, in preparation, she reached out to several seasoned directors for their advice. Jonze's was, "If you don't like a shot, just start turning off lights."

Most of us are not, nor do we necessarily want to be, Hollywood film directors, but we can all use that advice. If something feels off or wrong in your life, it's often because there's too much of something, not because there's too little. Too much of what? It could be anything. Our natural tendency is to create clutter to protect ourselves. We fill our lives with extra things—extra stuff, extra food, extra money. When something goes wrong, we add more. But more often than not, the answer is to have less. Less clothing, less crowding, less clutter. What's left under all that more is a simple elegance that might just be the answer. When you are overwhelmed by all the more in your life, just start turning off lights.

I've always been bad at listening, mainly because I've always thought I was really good at giving advice. I absorbed just enough information to process what someone was telling me and offer up a solution to their problem. I've since learned, largely from my patient girlfriend, that this method of "conversation" isn't really enjoyable or helpful for people—and giving advice is usually annoying unless it has specifically been asked for.

In hopes of confronting this bad habit of mine, I looked into what I could do about it. One analogy was particularly helpful: A good conversation is like a lock—not the kind that's on a door, but the kind that makes it possible to equalize the level of the water flowing in a canal. It is a gated enclosure. Opening and closing the gates allows water to flow from one lock into or out of the next, until the water level is the same in both locks. When it is, a ship can make its way through the canal.

Most of the time, people who vent in a conversation are not looking for solutions. Instead, they are hoping that venting to a quiet listener will lower the level of their anger, frustration, or some other powerful emotion so that they can move on.

# BE A LOCK

The answer, then,
is not an answer at all.
The answer is listening.

**IT'S NEVER REALLY LIFE-OR-DEATH** In discussing a risky choice I was preparing to make, I told my best friend that I felt like I was at a big, giant fork in the road. I could either stay in my office job and get a raise, or go freelance for a bit, branching out on my own. This choice was life-changing for me; its effects would ripple over my whole life—what my day-to-day would be like, my ability to pay my rent, my social network, my 401(k). I unloaded all of this on my friend, and her response was, "Go for it. It's not life-or-death."

I was surprised at first, but then I realized she was right. Choices are almost never life-or-death. Most of the time, we can bounce back from our choices if we need to; even if we fail, we can pivot. Robert Frost got us all worried that the proverbial "road less traveled" is the better one—that we could and might choose the wrong one, and that doing so would have terrible ramifications in perpetuity.

The truth, however, seems a lot simpler—if somewhat less profound. Sure, there are two roads, but whichever road you choose to travel on, you will eventually find your way, even if that means briefly going back the way you came. It's not life-or-death.

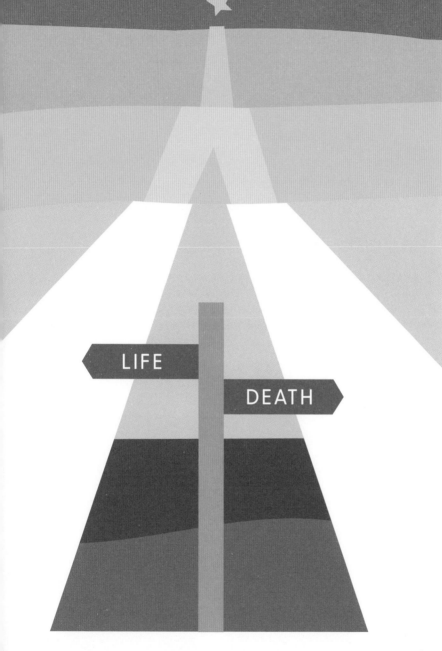

MAKE

NEW

Every
once in a while,
I wonder how people can
possibly continue to create new music—
after all, there are only so many notes and so many
ways to combine them. But lucky for all of us, there are combinations yet unexplored, melodies yet uninvented.

I am no musician, but I find so much comfort in that
thought. There will always be more to explore.
The same notes can always make
new music.

MUSIC

## TIME IS NOT REAL

Humans invented time. I'm not saying that time doesn't pass, that we don't age, or even that we don't have to abide by the system of time that we've invented. Rather, I'm saying that this system we live by actually has very little to do with our core being*ness*.

In his book *The Power of Now*, Eckhart Tolle posits that the concept of time is unimportant to our existence. He asks, if one day humans were gone from the earth, and only animals and plants remained, would there ever be a bird that said to another one, "What time is it?" The answer is no, of course not, because a bird doesn't need awareness of the hour to know what it needs to do.

You are the same. Though we've created tasks, schedules, and goals, none of that bears any relationship to what you are meant to do. Obviously, you cannot give up time altogether (not practically, anyway). But what if you take a vacation from time every once in a while? Maybe it's a few minutes, a few hours, or perhaps entire weeks where you simply let yourself *be*. Time will be there when you're ready to return—while it waits for no one, time *is* fluid, never-ending.

**AS IF** We've all had moments of doubt and uncertainty. Moments in which we tell ourselves stories of failure, in which we are so certain of poor outcomes that we don't even try. Our fear sabotages our chance of success before we've even made an attempt. In these moments, act as if.

No, I don't mean Cher Horowitz's favorite line from *Clueless*. I mean the cognitive behavioral therapy technique. All you have to do is act as if the thing you're most afraid of is exactly the opposite.

Act as if you are competent in your work. Act as if you will win. Act as if you are brave. Act as if the room is a better place for your having walked into it.

Sure, acting confident doesn't automatically make you confident, but that's not quite the point. The point is that, in acting confident, you are putting a stop to the automatic thoughts in your brain that tell you you aren't. You get a break from the story you're telling yourself in your head, and by acting as if, you give yourself a real shot at succeeding.

Act as if you are confident, worthy, valued, successful, and important.

**BABY KNEE-CAPS**

Someone once told me that babies don't have kneecaps. It's not true—they do, but their kneecaps are much softer than ours. Until children reach the age of three, their kneecaps are composed primarily of cartilage rather than hard bone. While they're learning to crawl, walk, and eventually run, they need a soft place to land—a practice kneecap, if you will. Children need time to grow, and their bodies happily give them that time.

But adults are still growing, too. Maybe you're learning a new skill, discovering a new point of view, or pursuing what you once thought was an impossible dream. All of that is growing. Your body may be old—or older—but your mind never stops being new to this world. Your mind, like a baby's kneecaps, is the perfect place to keep experimenting. Be grateful for your soft kneecaps. Use them.

# PUT YOUR STRESS IN A LIST

Anxiety is a manifestation of our stress-filled thoughts in a loop, playing over and over, and taking up valuable space in our brains. Anxiety is also the antithesis to creativity and clear thinking, which is why it's important to keep it at bay.

When I feel stressed, I make a list of all the thoughts taking up space in my head. And then, as much as I can I get on with my day. Write them down, put it to the side, and clear your mind of the constantly replaying anxieties. The list will hold on to it for you.

## THERE'S NO SUCH THING AS WRITER'S BLOCK

KT, a singer-songwriter friend of mine, and I were having a passionate discussion about why accessing creativity can be so difficult, when she told me she doesn't believe in the concept of writer's block. "It's a farce. Bullshit. If you can't write it's because you have nothing to say quite yet. In fact, you probably need to stop trying to write, and go out there and do something."

As a writer, I have leaned on the idea of writer's block from time to time as an easy way to avoid the responsibility of pursuing my work. Pretending that, because inspiration hasn't come to my doorstep, I must have nothing to say. But KT is right. If your words feel stuck, stop doing the same thing—stop sitting around and hoping something will change. Get up! Listen to music, read a poem, walk outside, or call a friend. And then write about it.

I didn't hear the phrase "the hill you choose to die on" until well into my adult life. If it's new to you, it refers to a thing you are willing to stake your bet on, put your energy toward, and fight for, no matter the cost. It's the most important thing to you—a thing you're not willing to budge on. The phrase comes up often in creative industries or places where lots of tiny decisions are being made all the time. Someone, usually your boss, project manager, or editor, will ask if whatever's at stake is the hill you want to die on—the point being that you die only once.

I wish I'd learned the phrase "the hill you choose to die on" a lot earlier in my life, because, as a young adult, I was willing to die on every hill. I wasted a lot of energy on trying to make every minor outcome go precisely my way—and nothing ever seemed to get done. Acting as if every decision is the most important one has the opposite effect: No one knows when something truly matters to you because you're too busy dying on every hill.

Clarify what actually is important to you and then spend your time and energy—and everyone else's—on only that.

**FIRST THEY'LL SAY NO**

Marie Curie—the godmother of radioactivity, the pioneer of women in science, and the first (and still the only) person to hold two Nobel Prizes in different sciences—was not initially allowed to study science. In Poland, where women were not permitted to pursue higher education, Curie was forced to enroll in an underground college in Warsaw called "the Flying University." Originally founded to educate women, the university became a safe haven for Poles living under oppressive Russian rule to study Polish history and culture.

A few years after completing her education and saving up money by working as a governess, Curie moved to France, where she was able to earn degrees in physics and mathematics at the Sorbonne. But even after she married and discovered radium (the element that remains the basis for modern cancer treatments), the Nobel committee still tried to exclude Curie from being considered for the prize, at first nominating only her two male colleagues. When her husband, Pierre, demanded Marie be included for her equal contribution, Curie became the first woman ever to become a Nobel laureate.

After Pierre died, Marie continued to study, and she received another Nobel Prize, this time in chemistry. She was the first female professor at the Sorbonne and the first woman to be enshrined on her own merits in the Panthéon of Paris. She was irrefutably one of the smartest and most consequential women who has ever lived. But at first, they said no.

## You will hear a lot of nos throughout your life.

These will come from people who don't understand your drive, believe in your mission, or stand by your right to pursue your dreams. They will tell you, like they did Marie Curie, that there is no place for your aspirations. Pay them no mind. First, they'll say no, but soon enough, they'll be at your door, clamoring for your contribution.

# ARCHES

I love the fact that, in architecture, arches are one of the strongest shapes. Bridges, cathedrals, castles, aqueducts, domes—arches are everywhere.

I love this fact because it proves you don't have to be hard and pointy to be resilient, strong, and beautiful.

You can stand
in your own
strength and
withstand
whatever forces
might come
toward you.

I don't draw. My sibling, Miggs, has always been better at drawing than I am, and so when I was around twelve, I stopped drawing because I don't like doing things unless I can be the best at them. In fact, my sibling is so good at drawing that they are a storyboard artist at Cartoon Network. At this point, it's safe to say that I will not be the best at drawing. Instead of stopping myself from drawing altogether, though, I've given myself permission to doodle. Yes, doodling is pointless in a way that drawing isn't, but actually, that's the point.

To doodle means to scribble absentmindedly. It is the art before the art, or maybe the art that will never become art. Doodling isn't supposed to be displayed or critiqued; it's done purely for the enjoyment and the expression that it allows. When I realized I would never be the best at drawing, I also stopped doodling at first, thinking of it only as a precursor to drawing and forgetting that some things are done just for fun.

Think about your life. Does it consist only of tasks you're absolutely sure you can accomplish? Routines you are good at, jobs you know you can do, languages you learned when you started to speak? We often stop ourselves from playing around in the things we don't know, because what's the point? But consider whether you've denied yourself pleasure, learning, or entertainment by needing to be an expert in everything you do.

Do some doodling today—
or whatever your equivalent activity
is. Do something not to get better at
it or to conquer it, but <u>because</u> you
have no idea how to do it.

## A TINY JOLT OF WONDER

I find day trips a simple reminder that you don't have to do much to change your circumstances. By definition, a day trip starts and ends right where you are, but with a secret slice of adventure packed in between. The memories from the day are a little treat you get to keep for yourself—when you get back home to where you've always been, no one is the wiser that you've been anywhere at all.

We all need to escape from our routines now and again. But so often, we don't get away because we're worried that in order to make an impact on our lives, we need a big break, a long trip, a vacation, or a getaway. But sometimes, all we need is the slightest change of circumstance, a tiny jolt of wonder to shake the sleeping self. Slip away for the day. Gain a new perspective on your old routine.

**FARTHER THAN THE SUN**

At my grandfather's funeral, everyone present sang an old Spanish hymn titled "Más Allá del Sol," which translates to "farther than the sun." The lyrics read, "I have a home farther than the sun."

I don't know where people go when they die—if they simply cease to exist, or if they go off to some place we don't know about in this life. I tend to think about death like physics: Energy can neither be created nor destroyed, just transferred. We're all made of energy, and when we die, we become some other kind of energy.

While I don't know who you've lost or how you lost them, I do know that we all, at some point, lose people we love. The feeling of missing them changes, but it never really goes away. When I feel the sun on my skin and experience a gentle warmth that can't be replicated by humans, a powerful reminder we're still alive, I think of my abuelo off somewhere "más allá del sol."

grief

Dawn

there is a soft morning light

so gentle

so beautiful

that it almost hurts the soul

for when have I ever been so gentle?

so generous?

### LIFE IS NOT BINARY

My perspective on life used to be binary. You were either good or bad, right or wrong, succeeding or failing, and there was nothing in between. So you can imagine that when I began to recognize in myself personal traits that were not so favorable, I started to despair. I immediately labeled myself a bad person who had been confused for all these years into thinking I was good. Here I'd thought I was kind and generous, when, in reality, I was just concerned with pleasing people. I'd thought I was altruistic, but perhaps I was entirely self-serving.

I wanted to change, but I found myself trapped in despair because I'd had all these bad traits within me to begin with—and that thought derailed me from any real progress. If I was a bad person, maybe I didn't deserve

**SHADES OF GRAY**

Bad to the bone

Running with the devil

Slightly sinful

to get better. If I was a bad person, maybe I couldn't get better.

Thankfully, friends and family graciously lifted me out of this dark place, reminding me that being all good all the time isn't realistic. My friend Kate put it perfectly, "Everyone's shitty, but everyone can be good and deserves love, too."

I learned in therapy that we've all picked up unhelpful patterns and responses throughout our lifetimes. The temptation is to believe these patterns are part of us or, worse, that they are the true us. In reality, they are just obstacles that prevent us from becoming the best versions of ourselves. We are neither entirely good nor entirely bad. Mostly, we are just people trying to be good while some unhelpful habits get in the way. When you know better, you do better.

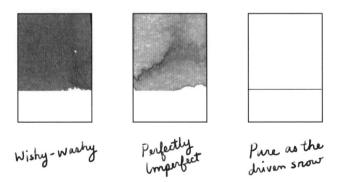

Wishy-washy    Perfectly Imperfect    Pure as the driven snow

**BAGEL ON A PLATE OF ONION ROLLS**

When I was growing up in the early 2000s, mainstream culture didn't showcase quite as many *different* women claiming their own space. My teen years were filled with images and music videos of Britney Spears and Christina Aguilera, skinny blonde women I knew I'd never resemble. This unattainable beauty standard made loving myself nearly impossible, because I couldn't see a way forward in the world as me. Despite being extroverted and seemingly confident, on the inside, I always felt just a little bit off. I felt different, unpretty, unremarkable, and altogether unworthy. I thought that if I wanted love, from myself and from the world around me, I would have to change who I was.

Then I discovered Barbra Streisand.

One day while with my dad in Barnes & Noble, I stumbled upon the discount bin with a collection of Barbra Streisand DVDs in it. I picked one up and asked my dad who she was.

"You've never seen *Funny Girl*?" he asked. "You would love it."

We brought home the DVDs and watched *Funny Girl* that night. From the very first song to the last, I knew I was changing. Streisand played Fanny Brice, a young Jewish singer with a booming personality who would eventually become a stage sensation—but not without everyone doubting her along the way. Everything she sang about captured exactly how I felt about myself. Just before the song "I'm the Greatest Star," she quips, "I'm a bagel on a plate full of onion rolls. Nobody recognizes me!" In that one moment, my entire existence was shaken. I, too, was a bagel on a plate full of onion rolls. Even though I thought I had something to offer, no one recognized me.

It may sound hyperbolic, but I know with complete certainty that, with that single sentence, Barbra Streisand as Fanny Brice paved the way for me to be myself. I felt seen, heard, and understood for the first time in my life. In that same song, she later yells, "You think beautiful girls are going to stay in style forever? I should say not! Any minute, they're gonna be out. Finished! Then it'll be my turn!" I was so overcome with relief that I laughed.

It's not easy to be yourself when those around you, especially in the public eye, make you feel like it's better to be someone else. But you must. Claim your space. Be a bagel on a plate full of onion rolls. The world may not be ready for your flavor yet, but, ultimately, others will thank you for bringing variety to the table.

Have you ever been in the shower and experienced a bizarre lapse in time for a moment where you can't remember whether you've washed your hair or not? If this has ever happened to you, more often than not, it's because you're not paying attention. Instead, your brain is off somewhere in la-la land, thinking about a stressful meeting you have in an hour or, even worse, replaying an embarrassing moment you had with your crush in sixth grade gym class. Either way, you're distracted. You are not present. This is the perfect moment to practice mindfulness.

Author and professor Jon Kabat-Zinn calls this the shower check. A moment to yourself to stop and simply ask, "Am I really here right now?" It may seem absurd, but if you start paying attention you will soon notice how often you aren't actually where you are. Sure, your body is here, but your mind is off somewhere else. Don't waste these moments. Be present. Check if you're really in the shower.

## FOR SUCH A TIME AS THIS

Despite not knowing exactly how I feel about the Bible, I have always liked the story of Esther, which appears in both Jewish and Christian traditions. In this story, Esther is a young Jewish woman who finds herself crowned the new queen of Persia, selected by King Ahasuerus as the most beautiful woman in the empire after his wife, Vashti, disobeys him. Esther quickly becomes the king's favorite, though she never reveals her Jewish background.

After Esther's cousin Mordecai refuses to bow to Haman, the king's highest adviser, Haman seeks and receives permission to kill all the Jews in the kingdom. Suddenly, Esther is the only one who can save her people—but she has to reveal herself in order to do so. Mordecai beseeches her to intercede, but Esther is afraid; if anyone approaches the king unsummoned, it's possible they'll be put to death. In an effort of encouragement and urging, Mordecai says, "And who knows but that you have come to your royal position for such a time as this?"

In the end, Esther listens to Mordecai, approaches the king (who is happy to see her), and saves her people.

As a child, I both loved and feared this story. *For such a time as this*—it might be my favorite line in all of literature.

But it haunted me. What time was it? Would I one day be called to my own "such a time as this"? I was overcome with the fear that one day, something bigger than me would call to me and I would have to be brave enough to sacrifice myself. Indeed, I worried we each had "such a time as this," and I worried more that I wouldn't recognize that time when it came for me.

It's difficult to know what it is we're meant to do here. None of us asked to be born, and so many of us spend our lives trying to figure out what to *do* with that gift we didn't ask for. We ask why we are here.

When we ask that question, we are essentially asking what Mordecai asked of Esther. "Have I come here for such a time as this?" In other words, what is the unique set of circumstances and characteristics that have brought me to this exact moment—and what am I supposed to do with them? How am I supposed to help? What am I meant for? It's daunting.

I really believe we each have a calling, a reason, a purpose. While that might not be to save an entire people, like Esther, it doesn't mean we aren't all meant for some special moment in history. We are. You are. Whether you know exactly why you are here, I believe you were put here for such a time as this—this very moment. You are capable of helping someone. No matter what you do or who you are, you can always help. Lean into the circumstances that have brought you to exactly where you are and lean into your life.

Besides housing more than 50 percent of the world's species, rainforests are spectacular for one special reason: They make their own weather. Water, in the form of vapor, rises off the leaves, trees, and plants in the jungle to create clouds overhead. When the clouds reach their capacity, they burst, spilling their water back down to the earth to replenish the rainforest's vitality and lushness. In this way, the rainforest nourishes itself.

# Make Your Own Weather

Everything you need to survive—to make, to create, and to live well—is already within you. Though support from those around you can be nourishing, you can do anything on your own. Even when it appears you have none, know that you have extra water hidden in your leaves. Make your own clouds, use your own clouds, and create your own weather.

## KEEP DREAMING, LADIES

I once attended an outdoor screening of *Jurassic Park* at the Hollywood Bowl during which the Los Angeles Philharmonic played John Williams's score live. It was, in fact, as cool as it sounds.

When the movie gets to the part where Jeff Goldblum gives his "God creates man, man destroys God, man creates dinosaurs" speech, Laura Dern responds, "Dinosaurs eat man. Woman inherits the earth." This line elicited cheers from all the women in the audience—and a guy sitting behind me was so bothered by this reaction that he felt the need to loudly yell, "Keep dreaming."

Yes, this man felt so insecure about his position of power that he couldn't stand the thought that women might get the chance to run things one day. While I'm certain he didn't mean it this way, I, too, would like to say, "Keep dreaming, ladies." The world is ours for the taking.

OAK TREES FROM ACORNS

EVERY
SINGLE
OAK TREE
YOU'VE
EVER SEEN
WAS ONCE
AN ACORN.
EVOLVING
TAKES TIME.

**nature** / you do you

While I was living in New York City in 2013, my morning walk to work included a street that was absolutely covered with stunning rose bushes. Without fail, though, I would be enjoying the gorgeous flowers one week, and the next there would be nothing but stubs. Every time the roses disappeared, I wondered why. Why trim something that appears to be blooming? Why kill something that still has life in it?

Roses, even those in peak bloom, have a season, with a time to grow and a time to lie dormant. As they near the end of this season, the ends of their stems begin to die, and disease starts to take hold within the buds. Without proper pruning, this can suck the life from the rest of the plant. Lacking the attention of a trim, even healthy rose bushes grow wild, expanding beyond their purview, rampant, without the support of a solid center. It seems counterintuitive, yes. But rose bushes need to be trimmed down to almost nothing in order to thrive when the next season begins. The trim signifies a time to regroup, recuperate, and ultimately replenish.

Often, the most difficult time to change or let go—to trim—is when we seem to be mid-bloom ourselves. We are thriving, or so we think. We resist the pruning because we can see only the current moment. We forget that there is a season of blooming ahead. But, just as I couldn't see what was going on with the rose bushes I passed on my morning walk, we might be blind to what's beneath the surface—what disease might have taken root in our stems, what expansion needs to be held back in order to support us in the future.

nature / self-improvement

# THINGS

## WILL

**ENTROPY**

IS THE GENERAL DEGRADATION

OF MATTER AND ENERGY

IN THE UNIVERSE

Entropy is the principle of thermodynamics that says everything around us is decaying. While that doesn't seem uplifting, I think, in some ways, entropy is a concept full of hope—because at its core, entropy is the promise that life, literally all matter in the universe, will continue to change.

The root of the word *entropy* comes from the Greek *trope*, which means "change," and *trepein*, "to turn." No matter how truly wonderful or deeply terrible life feels right now, know that it will change and turn—because it must.

# CHANGE

**BUTTERFLY GOO**    For most of us, butterflies were a component of one of our earliest science-class experiments, watching a mushy caterpillar build a cocoon and turn into a majestic winged creature. But what I didn't learn from that experiment, and what has altered my perspective on growth, is what happens inside the cocoon.

You see, caterpillars don't simply make a cocoon, slender down, and grow some wings. Rather, they disintegrate into what can only be described as "butterfly goo." That's right—somewhat grossly, the caterpillar releases enzymes that make it digest itself until nothing remains but its cells. After that, the cells begin reforming into disks that will eventually form all the parts of a butterfly.

I can't help but think that we, too, are like butterflies, and that meaningful change is not a superficial process that simply gives us wings. Change is, instead, a delicate disintegration of everything we used to be that makes us into who we will become. Real change, the kind that matters, sometimes means we must enter our own cocoon away from the pressures in the world, melt into goo, and reemerge.

If you're in the midst of painful growth, remember that from the messy, sticky goo comes a graceful butterfly.

science / growth / nature

**THE END** Through this project, I have learned—or, rather, reminded myself—that you can't force inspiration to pop into your mind. The number of days I sat down to work on this book, only to find my brain empty, was beguiling.

On one such day, I went for a walk around the block, searching for a spark. I found nothing, my brain as empty as when I had begun, but then, suddenly, a beautiful yellow butterfly emerged from the tree above me and slowly glided toward me until it was just out of reach. The moment was so beautiful, and so unexpected, that it made me cry. I hadn't been prepared to find beauty in that moment, yet there it was, a perfect gift for me.

What I've learned is that inspiration is almost entirely accidental. In fact, it is the novelty of inspiration that makes it what it is. Where there was nothing, something suddenly appears. Though you might put yourself in the path of inspiration, the most inspiring notion I can think of is that you never quite know what it is that will strike you.

Is it our obligation to seek inspiration then? I follow the poet Mary Oliver's instructions on this one: "Pay attention. Be astonished. Tell about it."

I hope this book has brought you new thoughts, new ideas, and new feelings. But, more than anything, I hope it has moved you to pay attention to the inspiration all around you. I hope you find your butterfly, and, when you do find it, I hope its beauty moves you to tears. Finally, I hope you share the inspiration you find and that it inspires others.

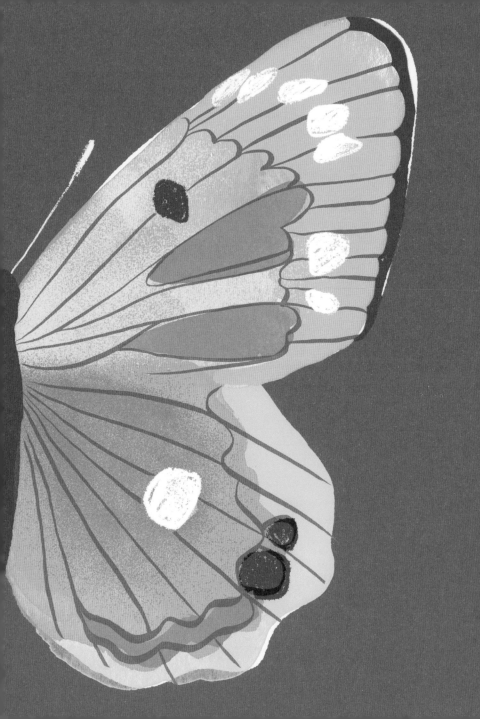

THANK
YOU FOR
READING